Italy:
Instructions for Use

Be sure to download our free companion publication,
Planning Your Adventure, available at **italyinstructions.com**

Italy:
Instructions for Use*

The Practical, On-site Assistant for the
Enthusiastic (Even Inexperienced) Traveler

by Nan McElroy

*When all else fails…read the instructions.

For information, please contact:

Illustrata Press
Atlanta, GA
+1 404 622 6786
press@illustrata.net
press.illustrata.net   or   italyinstructions.com

The author and publisher have made every effort to ensure the accuracy and completeness of the information contained in this book. However, we assume no responsibility for errors, inaccuracies, omissions, or any inconsistency herein. Any slights of people, places or organizations are purely unintentional.

Published by Illustrata Press, an imprint of Illustrata, Inc.
First printing 2004, revised 2007.

ISBN-13   978-1-885436-30-6   (ISBN-10 1 885436 30 0)

LCCN 2003114467

Printed and bound by Legatoria Editoriale Giovanni Olivotto in Vicenza, Italy.

Created, designed, and typeset on a Mac by Nan McElroy
using all Apple and Adobe products.

Open my heart and you will see
'graved inside of it: Italy.
Such lovers old are I and she
So it always was, so shall ever be

— Robert Browning

For the independent traveler, yet to discover their own Italy...

Acknowledgements

What would I do without my dear friends and colleagues, who have witnessed the evolution of my Italian life with reactions ranging from enthusiasm and understanding to confusion and complete mystification. Many have been generous with time and expertise when their own busy lives couldn't really spare it: Isa, Steve C, Graciela, Lucy & Tom, Bill and Pamela, Mali and Katie, Rebecca, Marjorie, Craig, all my Path buddies, Claudia McCue, Robert Wayne and, of course, all my relations (the mystified ones), still keeping those precious Kentucky home fires burning.

Questo piccolo vademecum è dedicato anche a tutti i miei carissimi amici italiani, gentili e pazienti, senza i quali non sarei mai riuscita a capire proprio NIENTE: la splendida ed incomparabile Gabriella, la mia carissima Mimma (dovete assaggiare la sua polenta col ragù; o magari una minestra di pesto Genovese; o i tortelloni con zucca e limone, oppure...mamma mia, si mangia bene da Mimma); il mio eroe Roberto, e la cara famiglia Gori (e il loro bel segreto di Certaldo Alto); Andrea, che capisce gli Americani, è vero, anche se non ci abita ancora; Mary, che non abita sempre in Italia ma è Italiana lo stesso; la solare Giuseppina, l'unica persona che conosco che può fare da mangiare *bene* a 500 persone; Lucia, che mi ha portato ad ogni angolo di Venezia, insieme con la sua bella famiglia Modolo, Ornella e Bruno lassù (finalmente); Stefania, che non critica più il mio Italiano come quando lei aveva sei anni; i ragazzi alla Rivetta (zitti voi!) che sanno benissimo cos'è una vera trattoria; ai miei primi insegnanti (guardate un po' quanto sono migliorata), agli amici nuovi, con tutto la loro Venexianità, chi mi sta rovinando la lingua corretta (la colpa vostra); Elena e Al, a chi voglio bene ancora; i ragazzi a Netarena a Bologna, il mio punto fisso tecnologico; e poi il mio amico perduto Cristian (ma dove sei andato?)

TABLE OF CONTENTS

❧ Planning Your Adventure

*Download the free pdf or the audio
podcast from italyinstructions.com.*

❧ In Italy

WELCOME to ITALY
Benvenuto In Italia

GETTING AROUND: By Car
or, Diesel is Not a Suggestion

GETTING AROUND: By Train
or, Leave the Driving to Them

GETTING AROUND: Other Options

GETTING AROUND: In Town

KEEPING IN TOUCH

Following the Instructions

Pronto! We've accepted the challenge. We're going to Italy. We're going on our own. We don't speak Italian, but we've practiced with language CDs; we've pored through guidebooks, reserved our hotels, cars, and train tickets, so we're all ready, aren't we?

Yes...and no. To discover all the Italy you possibly can in the brief time you have, you've prepared as time has allowed (after all, leaving the country for two entire weeks is no small feat). But here's the catch: *since you've never been, we guarantee you won't know all the questions you have until you actually arrive.* Once in Italy — because you're completely unfamiliar with the environment, language, and way of life — accurate and reliable information (and therefore understanding) can be much more difficult to come by.

Enter *Italy: Instructions for Use.* It's portable, well-organized, thorough, and current; designed to answer the questions you have when you have them, instilling you with the confidence you need to fearlessly explore Italy's nooks and crannies. We've tried to anticipate every question you might have as you travel, and then provide a clear, concise, easy-to-locate answer — so you can spend your time discovering and absorbing this most alluring country, instead of waiting for the bus that will never arrive because there's a strike today (which is why each person that passes keeps saying, "*Sciopero! Sciopero!*").

Our Instructions are always up-to-date. We now live in Venice, and have traveled throughout Italy for over a decade — sometimes alone, sometimes as a guide, sometimes with companions, Italian and American alike. We're always amazed at how quickly and to what degree things can change — as well as how others never do — so we're happy to pass along all the useful, often critical information we wish we'd had on *our* first visit.

Our guide is divided into two parts. The first,, *Planning Your Adventure*, is now a free download at italyinstructions.com. Make use of this section during the preparation stages, as you make all the decisions about where to go and when, what to take and what to leave, whether to drive or take the train, and more. Once you leave home, you most likely won't refer to this section again.

In Italy (the part you're holding in your hand) is divided into chapters pertaining to all the elements comprising your daily life there: traveling in a car or train, eating and drinking (*mangiamo!*), phoning home, finding the **duomo**. Keep it handy always

— then when you have a how-to or what-now question, just flip to the appropriate section to get the immediate assistance you need.

As you read, you'll notice two particular types of paragraphs scattered throughout the text:

> ❋ **WORTH NOTING** will inform you of particularly useful and little-known tips; and

> *ATTENZIONE* is designed to help you avoid the most common, often time-consuming pitfalls.

We've included vocabulary, listed in two ways. At the end of each *In Italy* chapter is a list of words in Italian with translation that you'll most likely use in the context of the chapter. Most of the same vocabulary is found at the end of the book, listed by the English words for quick reference.

Finally, there's the Appendix, which lists data resources in alphabetical order. If you're looking for a name, number, or Web site, check this section.

One section that we'd encourage you to review often, both before you go and while you're in Italy, is *Language: It's How You Say It*. It's not designed to teach you Italian, but instead to help you pronounce the Italian you do know correctly, and better understand what you'll hear in response to your questions. Any proficiency you take the time to acquire beforehand will be invaluable when attempting to communicate once you arrive, whether listening or speaking.

We've used lots of color throughout our guide not only to help you locate information easily, but more importantly, to convey the fact that in Italy, nothing, but *nothing* is black-and-white. You may notice extensive use of the words *usually, often, likely, frequently, sometimes, normally, may* and *perhaps*, while a word like *always* will appear far less frequently. Although we've written detailed guidelines based on personal experience and extensive research, to truly enjoy your time there, understand that in Italy, perhaps more than anywhere else, the exceptions *are* the rule.

One final note: You'll notice we refer to ourselves in the plural. This is hardly the royal **we**, but because I personally feel so indebted to all the assistance I've received over the years, from Italians and experienced travelers alike, it seems only right to refer to all of us who have, and are able to pass along, reliable, pertinent advice.

Personally, however, I wish you the very best of whatever Italy you choose to explore, and offer you *auguri calorosi per un bellissimo viaggio* (my warmest wishes for a wonderful trip).

Nan

If you're like most travelers, you're determined to learn what you can of the language before you board the plane. Perhaps you're taking classes, or listening to recordings as you drive. Too often overlooked, however, is knowing how *written* words are pronounced. This can not only make a big difference in how well you connect with the life and the culture, but also in how quickly you find the *duomo*.

It's *Bru-SKET-ta*.

Italians are used to strangers getting themselves in a pickle and needing a hand. They'll never judge you for inaccurate pronunciation, but likely have no idea that you're asking for the *Signa* (SEEN-ya) exit off the autostrada if you ask where the SIG-na exit is. Making a single word understood, and being able to glean the important information from the assistance you'll receive can mean the difference between asking for a scarf or a shoe, and finding that wonderful Tuscan restaurant recommendation, and having to drive home hungry and in the dark.

Pronunciation Keys: *La Pronuncia*

There's no word for "spell" in Italian. You instead ask, "How is it written?" Unlike English's endless exceptions, Italian is phonetically consistent: the way a word is spelled tells you how to say it, and vice-versa. Learn a few pronunciation rules, then, even if you have no idea what you're saying, you'll at least sound like you do!

What follows is a brief overview of the rules of pronunciation. As you prepare for your trip, revisit them at intervals until they come naturally to you — and they will.

THE VOWELS: *I Vocali.*

In Italian, each vowel has only one vowel sound, and there are no silent vowels. So for example, anytime there's an **e** at the end of a word, you pronounce it. That means *grazie* is pronounced *grat zee-eh*, not *grat-see*. So:

The vowel	is always	as in	or	which means
a	ah	ball	*mamma*	mother
e	eh	heh	*treno*	train
i	ee	bee	*vino*	wine
o	oh	bowl	*no*	no
u	oo	boon	*luna*	moon

That wasn't so bad, was it? Remember, every time you see one of the vowels above, they'll be sounded in exactly the same way: whether at the beginning, middle, or end of a word. As you listen to your language recordings, listen for the specific the vowel sounds: *a-e-re-o* (airplane).

THE COMBOS

Now it gets a bit trickier. To pronounce Italian words correctly, it's critical to understand that the sound of both c and *g* changes depending on what letter follows each of them. This is true for English as well, but unfortunately, much of Italian pronunciation is the reverse of what our native language-trained instincts tell us. The good news is that, as always, the pronunciation will be uniform, meaning the combos below will be sounded the same way every time they appear in any word. Get comfortable with these and you'll be well on your way.

C and G have one of two pronunciations: soft, as in *chair* and *gel*; and hard, as in *car* and *go*. When followed by i or e, the sound is *always* soft:

c	sounds like	"ch" as in chip
g	sounds like	"j" as in gin

Any other time, the sound of the c or g is hard, like *cab* or *gab* — including ch or gh. This means:

The combo	sounds like	as in	which means
ci	chee	*ciao*	ciao!
ce	chey	*centro*	center
ge	j	*gelato*	ice cream
gi	j	*giorno*	day
ch	kuh	*chiuso*	closed
gh	guh	*ghiaccio*	ice

Hang on. You can apply the very same rules to the **S**:

The combo	sounds like	as in	which means
sci	sh	*sciarpa*	scarf
sce	sh	*scelta*	choice

The combo	sounds like	as in	which means
sca	skah	*scarpa*	shoe
sco	skoh	*sconto*	discount
scu	skoo	*scusi*	excuse me
sche	skay	*scheda*	card
schi	ski	*schiuma*	foam

Don't give up. Here's the final hurdle. A **gn** or **gl** combination means you won't actually pronounce the g at all:

The combo	as in	is pronounced	and means
gn	*signore*	seen *yo* rey	sir, Mr.
	(ignore the g and put a y after the n)		
gli	*biglietto*	beel *yet* toh	ticket
	(Ignore the g and put a y after the l)		

※ WORTH NOTING: Italian nouns are never made plural with Ss, but instead either with *i* (which replaces the *o* for masculine words) or *e* (which replaces the *a* for feminine words). There are, of course, exceptions, but generally you can use this as a guideline.

For example, a popular destination in Tuscany that always presents a pronunciation challenge is *San Gimignano*, or *San Gee-meen-yah-no*.

For the language obsessed, here are some final hints. These are not as critical for your being understood, but good to know for your own understanding.

- **S and Z.** An s between two vowels is pronounced z, as in *museo*; a z will be sounded ts as in *pizza*.

The letter	as in	is pronounced	and means
s	*museo*	mu **zey** o *not* mus sey o	museum
	così	co **zee** *not* cos see	like so
z	*grazie*	**grat** sia *not* grassia	thank you
	inglese	een **gley** zey *not* eng glais say	English

- **qu** is pronounced qw (as in quick) just as it is in English, not k as in the Spanish pronunciation.

- **The meaning of a word is in its root.** Endings will change with the conjugation of verbs and pluralization of nouns, and as the word becomes an adjective or an adverb. In most cases though, your can refer to the root of a word for the key to its meaning.

Now, Tune Your Ear

Once you've begun to associate the pronunciation with how the word is written, practice pronouncing the vocabulary words at the end of the *Welcome to Italy* chapter according to the rules outlined here. Then once in Italy, listen for these words and phrases as you go about your daily Italian life: at the bar, on the train, in stores. They're little staples of the language that will help you integrate quickly, and give you your own opportunities to respond in a simple, but very Italian, way.

We won't specify the pronunciation of vocabulary words and complicated phrases in the rest of the manual, but instead indicate the syllable of emphasis with bold type and give you some key phrases here to get started. Review them according to the keys we've provided and you'll find you'll at least be pronouncing Italian like a native before you know it.

Ten Tips for the Traveler Abroad

Throughout more than a decade of traveling extensively (and now living) in Italy, we've assembled these suggestions from the many errors we've made, along with common experiences reported by and observed about Americans (as we are one), and other native English-speakers traveling abroad. There's a good chance many of these will apply to you, as they have to us.

☙ Leave the United States behind.

This sounds like obvious advice, doesn't it? Yet, we feel compelled to make it our number-one tip. If you're not a frequent traveler abroad, it can come as a shock that people do things differently elsewhere, for a variety of reasons, many of which we don't understand because *we don't live there.*

At home, we know what we like and can expect, feel perfectly comfortable demanding it and being accommodated accordingly. Once abroad though — especially in Italy — it's best to shift into discovery mode (oh, that out-of-control feeling) to get the most enjoyment out of your trip. If you instead adopt the "Let's see how good you are at giving me what I want" attitude (sadly, not uncommon), you'll surely be disappointed, and often. You might better travel to Switzerland or Germany, where order and logic reign supreme. . . or Florida.

☙ Book early to get that Room With A View.

There are two to four million of us traveling to Italy every year (along with eight million Germans, by the way), and all of us are reading the same guidebooks and researching the same Web sites for every charming twelve-room hotel from Venice to Palermo. If you're traveling from May to October, especially on a weekend, and you're not willing to do without a view, bathroom, or an ideal location, book lodging on your preferred travel dates as early as you can; then snag airline reservations later when you're comfortable with fare offerings.

☙ However much luggage you're taking, it's too much.

There's a common "take everything" approach that makes much more sense when you're loading up for a road trip than for traveling in Europe. Concentrate instead on efficiency — you'll be much happier unencumbered when navigating unfamiliar territory (even the Florence train station). You're not traveling to the Antarctic — you can always pick up the occasional item 'round almost any corner.

☙ Plan ahead for those experiences that are really important to you.

It's easy to create an expectation of the idyllic Italy we see in films, one in which we wander aimlessly to discover what our travel fate holds. If you have your heart set on a particular activity, though, waiting until the last minute to organize it will inevitably fail. You'll use your limited time trying to simply acquire information, something that can rarely be done expediently once in the country. Can we do a wine tour? (Yes, but it's booked up today, they don't offer it tomorrow, and you're leaving the next.)

Allow plenty of time to make plans, connections and decisions. Acquire appropriate maps and review them carefully before you drive (it won't help). Remember that it will be difficult to eat (well) after 2 P.M. and before 7 P.M., or find an attended gas station in more remote areas during lunch hour, or *ora di pranzo*.

✦ Don't try to see too much in too short a time, whether in one day or ten.

Remember, each time you change locations, you lose all or part of a day. Relocating always involves packing and preparation time the night before, the transfer itself, locating new lodgings and checking in, and getting oriented once again. Give yourself time to absorb what you do see, and allow time for rest and renewal. You don't have to see everything this trip; if you like it, trust us, you'll be back.

Try traveling with less of an intention to "do" a town, and more on finding a way to absorb a bit of the Italian-ness of it. Sometimes, we travelers have a tendency to quantify everything: How much did you see? Were you here or there or there? "We found the *very best* cantina" (out of thousands?), or, visited that famous butcher (that's right, Sting Was There). But, if you're looking to connect more with the culture itself, also look for opportunities to incorporate a bit of everyday Italy, and not just the prepackaged one. Perhaps you'll have a chance to visit an absolutely unknown coffee bar more than once — you'll be recognized the second time, without a doubt (then don't tell anybody where it is).

✦ Remember that Italy is a country, not a theme park.

Because there's so much to see, it's only natural to view Italy as having been created specifically as a tourist destination — it's been one for centuries. It's tempting to expect English translations everywhere, crystal-clear directions and signage throughout the country, along with opening hours convenient to our needs. Before you even begin researching airfares, understand that this will simply not be the case.

Italy is forever trying to refine the system that allows visitors to sightsee to their heart's content without destroying the "sight" in the process — which includes traditional Italian values, culture, and approach to life. The more you search for this authentic Italy, the more important it will be to surrender to whatever you find there.

In the same vein, remember that people in Italy are inhabitants with normal lives, not hired help looking for a tip. Is that what you would expect? These are not servants, just people of generous spirit. Tip professionals, and offer sincere thanks to anyone who helps you out of a jam.

✦ For Americans, this one fact can be the most difficult to accept: sometimes there's nothing to be done.

Operating in a strange environment can be a real test of your patience, but that's part of what we must expect when we travel. You'll inevitably encounter the irritating hitch here and there, usually when you least expect it. In these instances, it can be tempting to adopt a "Who's in charge here?" attitude, but trust us: your best strategy will be simply to *ask for help*. Pounding the counter or whipping out a credit card in an attempt to make something impossible materialize will get you exactly . . . nowhere. You'll be far more likely to receive the assistance you require if you take on the role of an honored guest, not a paying customer.

✦ Take a *deep* breath before drawing the conclusion that something doesn't work or isn't there, just because you're not familiar with it.

You've only been here a day or so, you're just over jet lag, and you've got a lot coming at you. Even if you're on a tight schedule, breathe once more; you're much more likely to find the answer you're looking for if you can search with a tranquil pair of eyes.

✦ Remember that there's always someone nearby who understands exactly what you are saying, good or bad.

As Mark Twain warns us in *Innocents Abroad*, "The gentle reader has no idea what a consummate ass he can become until he has traveled abroad." We Americans, for example, are known for our gregariousness (not a bad thing), and for speaking *ad alta voce*, and in our own expansive surroundings, we're not used to being overheard.

Take some time to read up on how things operate, double-check openings and closings, get the maps you need, and allow plenty of time to handle the unexpected, to avoid unintentionally insulting a mass of passersby in a moment of frustration in the more compact European environment — where almost everyone speaks some English.

✦ Make the pickpocket pick someone else.

When in transit, dress comfortably and simply, instead of like an unconsciously wealthy traveler who's just put a boatload of cash exactly where an unconsciously wealthy traveler might put it — ready to be pilfered by an experienced pickpocket who knows them all too well.

Leave your most expensive jewelry at home — it's just one less thing to worry about. If you're carrying lots of cash, put the bulk of it in a money belt that straps around your waist or hangs from your neck, or at least inside something that closes securely. Never keep all your money in one place, especially when in transit and in crowded tourist centers (popular piazzas, train stations, etc.), and *never* turn your back on your luggage or your purse.

Finally, remember that there is no amount of will, determination, or even cash that can force this delicious country — much like the aging of a good wine — to move at anything other than its own pace (that is why its artisans continue to flourish while they've all but disappeared from view here at home). Just see if you can switch gears a bit, let the culture seep into your pores, and see what you discover in the process.

In Italy

You know you're in Italy when...

. . . telling someone you live in an older building somehow loses its meaning.

Benvenuto in Italia

Hours of Operation

Traditionally, Italy is open for business from as early as seven in the morning until about 12:30 P.M. Much of the country goes home to eat and *riposare* until about 3:30 P.M., when it returns to work until 7:30 or 8:00 P.M. The lunch break, or the *pausa* (not *siesta*, which is Spanish), applies to businesses such as stores, gas stations, and perhaps even train stations in smaller towns. It does not include bars and other eating establishments, which after all is what you do during *l'ora di pranzo* (the lunch hour). Restaurants will instead close after lunch, and not reopen until 6 or 7 P.M. The exceptions are tourist centers (where there are simply too many people to turn away) and cities with a larger population such as Milan. Never expect Italy to be open on Sunday, but check in advance for exceptions.

The best approach to managing your own time is to plan for the standard opening hours, but then never be surprised at any departure from the norm. To avoid disappointment, or if you have any doubt, verify opening and closing times.

There are also seasonal fluctuations. Stores and offices may shut down for days or even weeks in August, when all of Europe traditionally goes on vacation. In addition, some tourism-associated businesses will close as early as November, through as late as February for renovations, revitalization, or just to regain a bit of sanity.

> ❧ WORTH NOTING: *Orario Continuato* indicates continuous hours, and means the business will remain open during the *pausa*.

Time, Dates and Numbers

TIME will most often be represented using the 24-hour clock, so 1 P.M. becomes 13:00, and 10:30 P.M. becomes 22:30. Often when speaking, Italians will say "Eight in the evening," knowing that makes more sense to us. But when it's written, the 24-hour clock will almost always be used. Just add 12 to anything from 1 P.M. on.

DATES will represented with the day first instead of the month, so 10/02/08 indicates the 10th of February, not October 2nd. To be safe, write the day and month as **10 May**, but do remember the standard format when you're reading a published date or one someone else has written for you.

NUMBERS will have commas where we put periods and vice-versa. So, the number 1,150.35 becomes 1.150,35.

Giorno di Chiusura (Closing Day)

Restaurants and small shops will likely have at least one *giorno di chiusura*, or closing day, when they'll take time off for business maintenance. These days and times will be unique from one business to another, and most often posted on their door. So, if there is special store or eatery you're particularly interested in, its best call ahead to confirm that they are, in fact, open.

In addition, many towns outside the tourist centers have a specific weekly morning or afternoon when almost all businesses close (excepting bars and restaurants). So if the *giorno di chiusura* is Thursday afternoon, and you want to buy a CD or do the grocery shopping on Thursday, you must do it before 12:30 P.M. To find out if there's a half-day when things will be closed where you're staying, ask at your hotel or the Tourist Information office (or at any business where you can find an English speaker).

Beyond that, plan on all normal businesses being closed on Sundays, and state-run museums being closed on Mondays. There are certainly exceptions, but verify them for yourself ahead of time.

> *ATTENZIONE:* Start familiarizing yourself with the way city and town names are written in Italian (*Firenze* instead of Florence, *Venezia* instead of Venice, *Padova* instead of Padua). You'll be more comfortable when reading, and be better understood when asking for information.

Economical Italy?

As Tony Soprano might say, "Fuhgeddaboudit." We often say that the only things that cost less in Italy are wine and a haircut; almost everything else can range from reasonable to costly to exorbitant, especially in more famous and popular destinations. If you're trying to trim a few Euros from the budget, making some of the following choices will help, and the quality of your vacation won't suffer in the least.

⬦ **Go off-season,** or *fuori stagione*. Lines are shorter for everything from museums to restaurants; airfares are cheaper and planes are less full. Except during major holidays such as Easter and Christmas, you should have no trouble finding bargains on lodging from the beginning of November through the end of March. (Keep in mind, however, that days are shorter, hours and closings become less predictable, and outdoor cafes retreat inside.)

✦ **Seek alternate, more remote destinations.** You'll get much more of a feel for the real Italy, and save a little money as well if you mix the all-too-frequent Venice-Florence-Rome itinerary with a place you've never heard of. Read up on Apulia (*Puglia*), for example, and see what you find.

✦ **Stay with the brothers and sisters.** Throughout Italy there are convents and monasteries that offer quiet, safe, spotlessly-clean lodgings and come in a surprising variety of forms, from modest to just shy of luxurious. Located in city centers and in the countryside, they'll often cost less than any comparable commercial lodging. (There may be a nightly curfew, but the hour will vary widely so be sure to inquire.) See Guidebooks in the Appendix for convent and monastery lodging references.

✦ **Take a chance on lodging that doesn't have a Web site.** They haven't had to pay the cost of development, and probably are not being frequented quite as much as a result. Whether a hotel, B&B or *agriturismo*, they'll likely cost less have more availability. Even bad web sites sometimes lead to good lodging choices.

✦ **Forego the toilet in your room.** This isn't nearly as undesirable an option as you might think. There's often still a shower and sink; only the toilet might be next door or across the hall. You may share it with one or possibly two other rooms — but very often it will be yours alone (*servizi privati esterni*) When you haven't booked ahead, making this occasional concession may also allow you to find a room when there otherwise may be no room at the inn.

✦ **Drink the house wine.** There are some truly excellent wines available throughout Italy, and if you're an enthusiast or an *intendatore*, do indulge anytime you can. But if you're on a budget, never be afraid to order *un mezzo litro* (half liter) of the house red or white. It will be younger, served in a carafe (*sfuso*), locally produced, and just fine, while costing less for a liter than we pay for a single glass at home.

✦ **Picnic to pinch a penny.** A deli (*alimentari* or *rosticceria*) and local fresh markets offer wonderful options for combining a broad selection of tasty ingredients to create a picnic to enjoy at the location of your choosing.

⟡ **Ask for water from the tap**. All of the water in Italy is safe to drink. Some taste better than others due to occasional heavy chlorination, however. Ask the waiter for his opinion, then order tap water (*acqua al rubinetto*), and spring for an extra *mezzo di vino sfuso* instead.

⟡ **Pay cash.** Using a credit card ensures that you'll be paying top Euro for whatever it is you're buying. Paying cash offers you the only possibility of a discount.

Dress Code

Italy is more, shall we say, attentive to dress than the U.S. is. You'll rarely see anyone shopping in athletic wear, for example, and you'll *never* see an Italian woman in shorts unless she is riding a bike or hiking in the Appenines.

> *ATTENZIONE:* In order to avoid being barred entry to a cathedral such as St. Peter's in Rome (you've come too far for that), always keep shoulders, knees and midriff covered. Keep an ample scarf or over-shirt handy if you'll need it.

That is not to say we must always wear our Sunday best. Of course, you'll be wearing a wardrobe that allows you to travel and sightsee comfortably, but try to respect local customs and mores in dress and behavior — especially in more conservative environments such as churches and public festivals.

The Smoking Thing

If you have a tendency to be appalled that everyone on the planet has not yet quit smoking, you may find yourself spending a good deal of your time abroad in a huff. Smoking is undeniably more common everywhere else in the world than in the U.S.; however, we notice that there are fewer people smoking all the time, and that people who do smoke seem to do so less frequently (and quite respectfully). The good news is that, in October 2005, smoking was banned in Italy everywhere but in private homes, open air, and spaces reserved specifically for smokers (head for IKEA for one of these). All hotel rooms are no-smoking rooms; the law pertains to all trains, bars, and restaurants, and has been welcomed by smokers and non-smokers alike.

There's no question that, as you travel, you'll be aware of more people smoking than you're used to; but even with allergies and more serious problems, you still may be able to manage it a better than you anticipate.

The Strike: *Lo Sciopero*

We couldn't begin to explain (or understand) the phenomenon of the all-too-frequent Italian strike, or *sciopero*. Suffice it to say that they occur, are publicized in advance, and can last anywhere from a few hours to a day or more. They manifest in various sectors such as transportation or communication, and may be national in scope, or limited to a specific city or region. They can also occur in sympathy with worker strikes in other countries.

To stay abreast of news concerning strikes that could interrupt your travel plans, check at the tourist office or at your lodging accommodations.

> ❀ WORTH NOTING: Even during a train strike, certain levels of service are still guaranteed.

La Dolce Vita

An Italian friend who works in one of those Venetian eateries with tables out in front reports, "You know, Americans never ask for help. I watch them pass through the *campo*, with all this luggage, their hotel directions in hand, back and forth, three, five, ten times. They must be exhausted, but why do they never ask for directions?"

I couldn't answer him.

OK, life is not always so *dolce* in Italy. Things can go wrong, especially when you're adventurous enough to explore this delicious country all on your own. When you do encounter the occasional, and inevitable, bump in the road, it should be easy enough to get the help you need, if you ask — Italians are by nature generous with their time and assistance.

> *ATTENZIONE:* Even when speaking English, enunciate your speech to be more easily understood.

This may not mean, however, that you'll always get precisely the resolution you're looking for. In Italy, in particular, there is simply no amount of cash-tossing or fist-pounding that will force a certain outcome. Best to save your effort, let someone know you have a problem, and be gracious enough to accept what assistance you find.

Of course, we all want to avoid travel bumps and bruises. But in the end, travel is an adventure, a time for discovery, and will ultimately involve some risk if you do it right. The best approach is to anticipate what you can, be as flexible as possible about the rest, and hope that somewhere in the middle you might find your own, personal version of what Hemingway described as "living all the way up."

Vocabolario

In conversation:

Grazie.	Thank you.
Prego.	If you please
Prego?	Pardon?
Per favore	Please
sì / no	yes / no
Certo.	Of course.
Forse.	Maybe.
Infatti	In fact.
D'accordo	I agree.
Mi dispiace	I'm sorry.
Scusi.	Excuse me.
Permesso	Permission (to pass)
Buongiorno.	Good morning.
Buonasera.	Good evening.
Mi chiamo Charles.	My name is Charles.
Molto piacere.	Pleased to meet you.
Parla Inglese?	Do you speak English?
Come va?	How's it going?
Come sta?	How are you?
Sto benissimo!	I'm very well!
A domani!	Till tomorrow!
Chissà.	Who knows.
Non lo so.	I don't know.
Non capisco.	I don't understand.
Penso di sì.	I think so.
Penso di no.	I don't think so.

May I help you? *(Mi dica.)*

Pronto?	Ready (to order, to go)?
Cosa volete?	What would you like?
Mi dica.	Tell me (May I help you?)
Ecco!	There! Here!
Vorrei...	I would like...
Potrei...?	Could I...?
Così? Così.	Like so? Like so.
A posto? A posto.	That's it? That's it.
Tutto bene?	Everything OK?
Tutto bene.	Everything's fine.
Va bene? Va bene.	OK? OK.
Arrivederci	Goodbye

Questions:

Chi?	Who?
Che? Che cosa?	What?
Quando?	When?
Dove?	Where?
Perchè?	Why? (Because...)
Come?	How?
Quanto?	How much?
Quale?	Which?

How Much? (*Quanto*?)		*mattina*	morning
molto / poco	a lot / a little	*pomeriggio*	afternoon
tanto / troppo	so much / too much	*sera*	evening
più / meno	more / less	*stasera*	this evening
piano	slowly, softly	*l'ora di pranzo*	lunch hour
veloce / lento	fast / slow	*mezzogiorno*	noon
		mezzanotte	midnight
Which? (*Quale?*)			
questo / quello	this / that	*presto*	early, soon
la prima	the first	*più tardi*	later
la prossima	the next	*ora*	hour
l'ultima	the last	*mezz'ora*	half hour
		minuto / minuti	minute / minutes
Where? (*Dove?*)		*pausa*	pause, or lunch break
avanti	forward		
davanti / indietro	in front of / behind	**How is it *(Com'è)?***	
destra / sinistra	left / right	*Mi piace.*	I like it.
diritto	straight	*buono / buonissimo*	good / the best
qui / là	here / there	*bello / bellissimo*	beautiful / most beautiful
sotto / sopra	above / below	*eccezionale*	exceptional
su / giù	up / down	*stupende*	stupendous
vicino / lontano	near / far	*splendida*	splendid
		incredibile	incredible
When (*Quando*)?		*perfetto*	perfect!
domani	tomorrow		
ieri	yesterday		
oggi	today		
giorno	day		

Hotels & lodging (*Alberghi e l'alloggio*)

una camera	a room (chamber)
singola	single room
doppia	double room
tripla	triple room
con bagno	with bath
con doccia	with shower
letto matrimoniale	with double bed
letti separati	twin beds
notte / notti	night / nights
affittasi	for lease, for rent
completo	no vacancy
disponibile	available
periodi brevi	short stays
portobagagli, fachini	porters
prenotazione	reservation
prezzo	price
tariffa	fare
asciugamani	towels
asciugacapelli	hair dryer
carta igienica	toilette paper
chiave	key
coperte	blankets
guanciali	pillows
ferro da stiro	iron
fumare	to smoke
giorno di chiusura	closing day
orario continuato	no pause
sciopero	strike

Days of the Week

lunedì	Monday
martedì	Tuesday
mercoledì	Wednesday
giovedì	Thursday
venerdì	Friday
sabato	Saturday
domenica	Sunday

Friends and Family (*Amici e la famiglia*)

uomo	man
donna	woman
signore, signori	sir, gentlemen
signora, signore	ma'm, ladies
mamma	mother
papa	father
marito	husband
moglie	wife
sorella	sister
fratello	brother
figlio, figlia	son, daughter
nonno, nonna	grandfather, mother

Colors (colori)

nipote	grandchild, niece, nephew	*azzurro*	turquoise
		bianco	white
cugino, cugina	cousin	*blu*	blue
zio, zia	uncle, aunt	*giallo*	yellow
cognato, cognata	brother, sister-in-law	*marrone*	brown
suocero, suocera	father-, mother-in-law	*nero*	black
		porpora	purple
nuora	daugher-in-law	*rosso*	red
genero	son-in-law	*rosa*	pink
		verde	green
		viola	violet, purple

Numbers

uno	1	*undici*	11	*dieci*	10	*cento*	100
due	2	*dodici*	12	*venti*	20	*duecento*	200
tre	3	*tredici*	13	*trenta*	30	*trecento*	300
quattro	4	*quattordici*	14	*quaranta*	40	*quattrocento*	400
cinque	5	*quindici*	15	*cinquanta*	50	*cinquecento*	500
sei	6	*sedici*	16	*sessanta*	60	*seicento*	600
sette	7	*diciasette*	17	*settanta*	70	*settecento*	700
otto	8	*diciotto*	18	*ottanta*	80	*ottocento*	800
nove	9	*diciannove*	19	*novanta*	90	*novecento*	900
dieci	10					*mille*	1000

. . . your server speaks at least two more languages than you do.

or, Diesel is Not A Suggestion.

Il Traffico

On her first visit to the U.S. from Florence, our Italian friend's sister was struck by the apparent order she found on the roads. "My," she commented, "American drivers certainly are disciplined." She was noticing how almost everyone drove at a reasonable speed, stayed in their own lane; and how at red lights, what motorcycles there were stayed in line behind the cars, instead of swarming to the front to get ahead of them. In contrast, according to another friend's description, Italians "drive like the devil, without rules, but with great intuition and skill."

In the United States, "traffic" consists of hordes of individual drivers, each of whom seems to believe that the road belongs entirely to him. In Italy, *il traffico* is an entity in and of itself: you enter it as you would any other type of community, and abide its unspoken rules for as long as you are a part of it. We can't really prove it, but our theory is that Italian drivers — from the schoolboy on his *motorino* to the grandmother zipping about in her VW Golf — are endowed with an innate radar and some extraordinary type of hyper-extended peripheral vision, that allows them to successfully anticipate any move that anybody in a fifty-meter radius could potentially make.

When you're crossing the road on foot, and a Citroën Xsara comes within a *centimetro* of swiping you as it rounds the corner (it's true, you would've been a pancake in the U.S.), the temptation is to stomp your feet, raise your fist and curse vociferously at the rapidly receding bumper. What you don't realize, is that the Xsara *never even came close*. These drivers know their cars, the roads, and how to drive exceptionally well.

This is the environment in which you'll be operating if you so choose, and when it doesn't completely wig you out, it's great fun. No Italian will cut you off if he thinks you know where you're going (use your blinker!), but neither will she sit patiently and wait for you to make up your mind. The sooner you decide not to take any of this personally, the sooner you will begin to enjoy yet another aspect of your Italian adventure. Just put your car behind another car that you think is going where you're going and...*Avanti!*

Types of Roads

The *Autostrada*

Just as for a U.S. Interstate, *autostrada* expressways are indicated by large, green signs (although their design is somewhat different). They're identified with an **A** followed by a number (such as the **A1**, which runs from *Milano* to *Napoli*). There are also specifically-named bypasses that circumvent city centers or connect one *autostrada* with another. In Rome, for example, there's the **Grande Raccordo Annulare**, or G.R.A., that encircles the city; in Bologna, the **Tangenziale** connects A1, A11 and A13.

One difference between Italian expressways and our own Interstate highways is that all *autostrade* are toll-roads. You'll take a ticket when you enter the toll-way, and present it to pay when you exit, the toll being calculated by how far you drove. Some sample tolls:

Venezia	->	Firenze	€14
Firenze	->	La Spezia	€10
Milano	->	Verona	€8
Firenze	->	Napoli	€24
Roma	->	Napoli	€12

(See the *Travel Times and Cost Estimates* table at the end of the Appendix for more information.)

You may pay tolls with cash or credit card at attended or self-service booths, or by credit card in the *VIAcard* (not *Telepass*) self-service lanes — look for the credit card logos. If you ever have any problem in the self-service lanes, press the *richiesta di intervento* button and wait for assistance.

If you'll be doing a significant amount of traveling on the *autostrade*, you may want to consider the purchase of a pre-paid *VIAcard* in denominations of 25, 50 and 75 Euro to simplify your toll-way life. *VIAcards* are sold at *Punto Blu*, at attended toll-booths, at *Autogrill* restaurants, in the service center gas stations, and in many *tabaccai*.

Service centers (*Area Servizio*) are dotted all along the *autostrade* and resemble our Interstate rest stops, in that when you exit them you're able to return only to the expressway. They offer significantly more services, however. You'll find gas stations (always open), food (from snacks to full meals), a *Bancomat*, hotels, showers, and camper services. See the Appendix for web sites with lots of specific *autostrada* info.

※ **WORTH NOTING:** Along the *autostrada*, signs with distances to destinations will appear in the center median.

The *Superstrada*

Indicated by blue signs, a *Strada di Grande Communicazione* or *S.G.C.* is very often a fine alternative to the *autostrada*. Like *autostrade*, they are four-lane, divided expressways and so move rapidly, require no tolls, and can also be more scenic. These roads are especially good for avoiding the *autostrade* on summer weekends (when they can come to a complete standstill as vacationers pour back in from the beaches) or whenever you might prefer a more interesting drive to the absolute fastest route.

Main Roads: *Strada Statale* and *Strada Provinciale*

These are primary highways: two-lane roads that follow routes that have connected towns and communities throughout the Italian countryside for centuries. They're not always clearly marked (although a *strada statale* will be indicated by the initials **SS**); you'll be much more likely to use signs pointing the direction from one town to another for finding your way, than an actual highway marker. It's much more critical when traveling these roads to have an excellent map and follow it closely... unless you'd rather throw caution to the wind and see where it blows you.

❋ WORTH NOTING: If you're using Touring Club Italiano maps, the green lines along specific stretches of roads will indicate particularly evocative scenery and are worth seeking out. Look for similar notations on other brands of maps.

Secondary Roads

Called *strade bianche* (white roads), they're not the most comfortable, and rarely paved. They're great for adventuring though, or finding out if a short cut really is shorter.

ATTENZIONE: Use extra care when judging time and distance on country roads. Squiggly lines mean curves and hills, and can increase driving times significantly, especially if you miss that tricky turn.

Road Signs

Italian road signs can be just different enough from what we're used to seeing to be confusing now and again. Best to take some time to familiarize yourself beforehand to reduce confusion down the road (so to speak).

The signs come in five fundamental versions, represented in the following figures. Each one has a general meaning, with specifics graphically represented in the center. Almost all of the driving indications you'll see will fall into one of these categories. Look for a variety of common signs at the end of this chapter.

RED CIRCLE: *Not allowed*
Restriction
Represented by a center grafic: entry barred for certain types of vehicles, no passing, or other action; a number indicates speed limit.

BLUE ARROW: *You must*
Imperative Action
This arrows indicate a one-way street, or the *only* direction you may turn.

RED TRIANGLE: *Attention*
The graphic in the center is international and fairly self-explanatory: curve, cross-walk, train crossing, slippery road.

RED TRIANGLE, reversed: *Yield*.
Look familiar?

RED TRIANGLE, yellow ctr: *Warning*
Construction, emergency or other temporary condition, illustrated with a center graphic.

At intersections of main roads, you'll often see a plethora of indicational signs stacked one over another. Some will have associated graphics to aid in deciphering them:

- **BLUE** - cities, towns, *superstrade* and parking.

- **WHITE** signs for civic information (the center, the train station (*Ferrovia*), soccer stadium, hospital, pharmacy, police). You'll always spot a graphic and an arrow.

- **BROWN** and YELLOW for businesses, including hotels, restaurants, spas, vineyards and other commercial and private enterprises.

When approaching an intersection, it can be truly harrowing to try to locate the sign for Siena among the twenty other blue destination signs, while all of *Firenze* is on your bumper. There's unfortunately no simple solution: recruit the assistance of your passengers, pull over so that others may pass (use your blinker), ask for assistance from passersby.

> ✤ **WORTH NOTING**: When you enter a town, you'll see a sign with its name. As you're leaving it, you'll see the same sign with a diagonal red bar across it.

Parking

It's not driving in Italy that's the biggest challenge, it's parking in Italy. There are many more cars than places to put them, and a parking space can not only be hard to come by, but expensive to boot.

When visiting historic centers, you'll most likely park in a lot or garage, indicated with a white P on a blue background. Garages and parking lots operate much like they do here: you'll take a ticket as you enter and pay as you exit.

> *ATTENZIONE:* Take note of how you'll pay for parking. In some garages and lots you must pay a cashier (*cassa*) *before* you return to your car. If you arrive at the lot exit without a paid ticket, you won't be able to open the gate, and may prevent others from exiting too.

If parking on the street, pay attention to the stripes on the road. Colored lines indicate whether or not you're allowed to park (white or yellow), and whether or not parking is paid (blue). To avoid a ticket that will follow you all the way to the rental-car bill, carefully review local parking rules with your hotel or the tourist office.

Depending on the region, street parking may be paid for either by purchasing a *gratta e sosta* (scratch and

park) ticket at a *tabaccaio*, or by purchasing a ticket issued from a meter box located on the streets where paid parking is available. Scratch and park tickets are good for specific periods of time: you'll indicate the time of your arrival by scratching appropriate squares and placing the ticket on the dashboard. A parking ticket purchased from a machine on the street will have the time stamped on it when it is issued.

> ※ WORTH NOTING: If you find a parking space with a time limit (*zona disco*), find a piece of paper, write the time you arrived on it, and place it on the dashboard.

Car Rental Reminders

If you rent a larger car, it will often be a diesel version. They're far more common in Europe than in the U.S., and are more economical on fuel. So, before you leave the rental office, make sure you know which type of car you have: the results of filling up with the wrong type of fuel can be... inconvenient at the very least.

Picking up or dropping off a rental car at an airport is not much different than anywhere else. If you're considering a non-airport location, review the following reminders.

✧ **When picking up your car, be sure you know what rental office you'll be looking for.** If you rent through a broker such as AutoEurope, they'll book your car through one of several European or American rental companies (Avis or Europcar, for example). There are office locations for all these companies all over Italy, both at airports and in town centers, so be sure you understand which company you're in fact renting from. There may not be an AutoEurope sign, but the specific rental agency sign instead. You'll look for this same agency when you drop the car off, even if it's in a different location.

✧ **Before returning your car, it will help to know the exact location of the car rental office.** Airports are no problem, but if you have a city location in a town even as large as Orvieto, you could waste a considerable time searching for the rental office in an ancient center in intense traffic and narrow, one-way streets. The people who rent you the car will likely only have an address — they'll have no idea how to get there. And no matter how well the folks at the rental office speak English, it's best not to rely solely on them to give you directions. Get a map, make a dot, and call the rental office before you leave if you have any specific questions (their English will be fine).

✧ **Make sure you have the correct opening and closing hours of the rental office.** Airport offices have long, continuous hours (one reason pickup costs more): not so for city offices. Note the hours on your voucher and with your rental agent, and confirm them with the local rental office the day before, especially if your schedule is tight or it's a Saturday or Sunday pick up or drop-off. If you arrive late to return a car and the office has closed, there will be nothing to do but leave the car — for which you'll be charged an extra day (or two).

※ **WORTH NOTING:** Depending on the distance, you may or may not pay a surcharge to pick up in one location and drop off in another. Outside Italy there will be a surcharge, but it's still an option.

Filling Up

Italian cars are extremely fuel-efficient, so depending on how much you'll be driving, you may not refuel more than once. Gas prices run approximately €1 per liter, or about $5 per gallon, so it can easily cost $60 or more to fill your tank.

Here are a few fundamentals to keep in mind:

- Gas stations are always open on the autostrada, and open longer hours on the Superstrada (S.G.C.).
- There are not as many gas stations in Italy as there are in the U.S., so if you plan on refilling off the *autostrada*, it's better to do it sooner than later.
- Gas stations in town and on the highway may be closed midday, and may also have a *giorno di chiusura*.
- There are self-service pumps available at many stations when they are closed (plan to pay cash), although there are many different designs and can be confusing to use.

☞ **WORTH NOTING**: To fill up at an attended station, just say "*Il pieno* (full), *per favore.*"

When using self-service pumps at unattended stations, it's not always possible to use a credit card, but the machines will sometimes accept a cash card. They always accept cash (*bancanote*). To use a self-service pump, the overall process will be as follows:

- **Pay first.** Insert bank notes or a cash card. If using cash, you'll see the amount of credit displayed in the window on the pump. If you're using a cash card, you may enter an amount, or fill-up by entering nothing.
- **Select the type of fuel**: *gasolio* or *blugasolio* for diesel, *senza piombo* for unleaded gas, and confirm.
- **Remove the nozzle and fill**. Don't remove the nozzle until after you've selected the type of gas, or the pump won't function properly.

There are also self-service pumps at attended stations, but instead of paying beforehand, you'll pay the attendant with cash or credit card once you're done.

ATTENZIONE: To avoid an embarrassing call to the rental car company, make sure you know what kind of gas you need and the correct name for it. The nozzle size won't prevent you from putting diesel in a no-lead tank, or vice-versa.

Rules of the Italian Road

Tap-tap. Many roads are quite old and very narrow, both in historic centers and in remote country or mountain roads, such as those around Como or the Amalfi coastline. To avoid a potential fender-bender, it's customary to tap your horn to signal your approach to blind corners and curves in one-lane roads and alleys.

Stay to the right. Driving on the autostrada is just like driving on the interstate in the U.S., with one notable exception: if you even think of dawdling-about in the left-hand lane, at least seventy-five Alfas will materialize in your rear window, with headlights flashing, and continue to hover there until you *move to the right. Capisce?*

After *you*. If I'm an Italian who makes a particular drive several times a week, you're probably the twentieth tourist that day that I've had to follow at a snail's pace because you're either admiring the scenery, or trying to drive and read the map at the same time. So, out of courtesy, flip on your blinker and put your two right tires over on the shoulder — they'll take care of the rest. (Oh, and the speed at which they pull away doesn't indicate any irritation. It's just how they drive).

> *ATTENZIONE:* Roundabouts (*rotonde*) are appearing in droves as Italy searches for ways to keep traffic moving. When entering a roundabout, remember to yield to traffic already inside it. Once you're inside, you have the right-of-way over incoming cars.

One-way (*Senso Unico*); this way only
White arrows on blue background.

Parking; Parking Lot

Curve Ahead   No Outlet   Not Allowed   Do Not Enter   Yield   No Stopping or Parking
Vehicle types, passing, etc.   (Divieto di Sosta)
(blank, no vehicles). Speed Limit.

Vocabolario

Vehicles and their parts:

bicicletta	bicycle
macchina, veicolo	car, vehicle
moto	motorcycle
motorino	motor scooter
gomme	tires
targa	license plate
porta	door

Driving and parking:

ascensore	elevator
cassa	cashier
garage	garage
gratta e sosta	scratch and park
parcheggio	parking lot
parcheggio a pagamento	paid lot
posto	place
sosta	stop (park)
tessera	cards (of monetary value)
zona disco	disc zone (paid parking)

On the road:

bivio	fork (division)
cartello	sign
galleria	tunnel
noleggiare	to rent (a car)
richiesta di intervento	request for assistance
segnale	signal
semaforo	traffic light
sorpassare	to pass
strada	road
via/viale	street

Do this, do that:

direzione	direction
indicazioni	directions (instructions)
ingresso, entrata	entrance
proibito, divieto	prohibited, forbidden
divieto sostare	no parking
passo carraio/carrabile	keep clear/loading zone
rallentare	slow down
senso unico	one way
tutte direzioni	all ways
uscita	exit
vietato	forbidden

Finding your way:

Dov'è...	Where is...
Ci siamo persi.	We are lost.
cartina, piantina	map
est	east
ovest	west
nord	north
sud	south
avanti / davanti	forward / in front
dall'altra parte	on the opposite side
diritto	straight
destra	right
indietro	behind / backward
lontano	far
sinistra	left
vicino	near

Road conditions and weather:

coda, fila	line (traffic back up)
nebbia	fog
pioggia, piove	rain, it's raining
vento (forte)	wind (strong)
ghiaccio	ice
neve	snow

At the gas station:

benzinaio	gas station
benzina	gasoline
fare la benzina	to get gas
non funziona	it doesn't work
olio	oil
il pieno	fill it up

Types of gas:

benzina verde or *senza piombo*	unleaded
gasolio	diesel
blugasolio	diesel, no sulfur additives

Filling up (self-service):

attendere	wait
accostare la banconota	insert the bill
estrarre la pistola	remove the fuel nozzle
Fai da te	do it yourself
fuori servizio	out of service
massimo importo	maximum amount
non da resto	doesn't give change

. . . you want to go somewhere, and you can take a train to get there.

GETTING AROUND: By Train

or, Leave the Driving to Them

Unless you live in the northeast or perhaps the northwest, you probably do very little train travel. The train system serves Europe and Italy very well, however, and the more familiar you are with how it works, the better it will serve you. If you'll be based in a city of any size at all, you'll find the train a very convenient way to visit nearby destinations for the day, and overnight.

The train system in Italy is federally owned and operated. FS stands for *Ferrovia dello Stato*, or State Railroad. Its structure resembles an airline system: the regional hubs are in principal cities such as Rome, Milan, Bologna, Florence, Naples; and local trains depart from these hubs to smaller, more remote destinations. TrenItalia is the commercial branch of the Italian railway, they handle the sales and service end of the system.

By the way, you won't be the last traveler to watch your train ease out of the station, arriving only moments after the scheduled departure time, having mistakenly assumed that because the trains are Italia, the schedules are probably a bit lax. *Not.*

Types of Trains

Trains can be divided into two categories, classifiable by speed, comfort and amount of distance they cover. National trains are faster, cushier, quieter, and designed for long-distance travel, connecting all major cities in Italy. They include the top-of-the-line **Eurostar** and super- fast **EurostarAV** (*Alta Velocità*) models, the **InterCity** (the distance train prior to the Eurostar, known as the **EuroCity** when its destination is international), and its completely updated, remodeled cousin, the **ICplus**.

Seat reservations are required for Eurostar, Alta-Velocità and ICplus tickets; IC reservations are optional (but recommended to avoid having to sit in the corridor during busy periods). You'll pay no supplement with your rail pass on an IC, but the trains run less frequently.

Regional trains run on routes that connect larger hubs with local and regional destinations, and are frequently traveled by commuters, students, and tourists alike. *Regionale*, *Diretto*, and *InterRegionale* (R, D, and IR) trains are economical (tickets rarely exceed €10) and unreservable. **IR** and **D** trains may have AC and first class cars, not so for *Regionale* trains. Regional trains stop more frequently, but the journey will rarely exceed an hour. These are the trains from Florence to Lucca, for example, or Rome to Viterbo.

Additional trains include: *T-Biz*, fast trains serving Milan - Bologna - Rome geared to business travelers; and *TrenOK*, low cost connections from Milan to Rome, and Rome to Bari, reservable online, through the call center, and using self-service machines only.

The following is a summary of train characteristics:

TRAIN	DESCRIPTION	RESV.	AC	CLASS
NATIONAL (long-distance)				
FB	Super fast	Req.	Yes	1-2
ES★	Hi-speed	Req.	Yes	1-2
ICplus	Fast, updated	Req.	Yes	1-2
IC	Fast	Opt.	Yes	1-2
REGIONAL				
R	Connects regions	No	Likely	1-2
D	Faster, fewer stops	No	Maybe	1-2
R	Local; most stops	No	Not likely	2

The night trains include the *InterCity Notte (ICN)*; and the *EuroNight (EN)*, and offer a variety of sleeping accomodations from functional to luxurious, in both first and second class, depending on the final destination and the length of the journey. All but the most adventurous of travelers should probably avoid the *cuccette*, or open sleeping compartments; other sleeping accommodations range from quite acceptable to posh. (The *Espresso*, *E*, is a long-distance, budget night train...but not for the faint of heart.)

Which Class?

The primary differences between first and second class are price, space and number of people. The contrast between first and economy class in an airplane, however, is more drastic than on any train. The ticket price is notable, and can make a considerable difference in a Eurostar-for-four journey. (First-class Eurostar tickets cost about 45% more than second-class; for other trains, the percentage of increase is less, as is the cost of the ticket.)

First-class cars will contain mainly American tourists and European business folks; second class, everybody else. If you're not traveling a great distance and you'd like to save a few Euro, you'll be perfectly comfortable in second class. If you'd rather hear a little more English spoken around you, prefer electric seats, or if it's a long journey, first class might be your choice. (If you're traveling with a lot of luggage, you'll certainly feel less conspicuous there).

> ❧ **WORTH NOTING:** Take your bike on trains where you see the bicycle symbol for a €3,50 supplemental fare or the price of an extra ticket. 🚲

Ticketing and Reservations

You can think of the ticket categories as having two divisions, just like the trains themselves. The first type of ticket is for distance trains, specifying departure and arrival destinations, and offering reservable seats; the second division is for regional trains, and reflect distance (*chilometri*) as opposed to destination. As long as where you're going is within the distance specified on your (validated) ticket, you're good to go.

You can purchase train tickets in a wide variety of ways: on the *TrenItalia* web site (up to two months in advance, www.trenitalia.com), from an online site or travel agency (commission applies), at an Italian travel agency (at cost), at a train station the ticket counter or self-service machine, or by calling the TrenItalia Call Center, **89 20 21** (a toll call, only in Italy). Buy regional tickets also at a nearby *tabaccaio* or newsstand.

> ❧ **WORTH NOTING:** National trains can be booked Ticketless on the TrenItalia web site; regional tickets cannot (but can be purchased and the pulled from self-service machines).

The train system is highly utilized: by Italians, tourists, and everyone in between. Trains can fill up quickly on popular routes, during peak tourist periods, and Italian holidays. We mean literally: without a reservation, you may be able to board, but have no place to sit. Trains that require reservations are meant to prevent this situation, but this means that without a reservation, you'll be unable to board at all.

Whether you purchase your tickets in advance or wait until the last minute will depend on several things: how confident you are of where and when you want to travel, whether it's necessary or possible to reserve, how crowded you expect the train to be, and whether you just prefer to get things out of the way.

If you need to buy a ticket or make a reservation at the station before you travel, give yourself some extra time, especially at principal stations during tourist season. Better yet, stop by any travel agency near where you're staying the day before (ask your hotel for a nearby agency).

> *ATTENZIONE:* To ensure your seat on a fast train (especially if traveling in a group in first class), book a minimum of two days in advance. During peak periods, it's not unusual to try to reserve for same-day travel and have to sit separately...or to find the train full.

If you've arrived at the station without a ticket and/or reservation, but see a train ready to depart for your destination, find a conductor in the green *FS* jacket and tell him you have no ticket but you'd like to take this train. If there are seats available, he'll give you a car and seat number (write it down if you need to) and board the train. Once the train departs, he'll come by and collect for the ticket and reservation. **Note that there will be an €8-per-ticket surcharge for on-board purchase, and the conductors can only accept cash.** No cash...no ticket.

> *ATTENZIONE:* If you get on a Eurostar train without a reservation and do not notify a conductor immediately, the "surcharge" will turn into a hefty fine.

SELF-SERVICE TICKETING: Two Versions.

The **Self-Service Ticket Vendors** — for travel within Italy — can be the simplest, most convenient, least time-consuming way to purchase, reserve, and even validate a ticket. You can obtain train schedule information from them as well.

Just like the trains, there are two categories of ticket vending machines. The big, yellow and gray older models, and newly-redesigned teal versions issue any type of ticket, and are scattered throughout stations where distance trains pass. They're convenient, have touch screens that speak six languages, are intuitive to operate, take cash and credit cards, and usually have much shorter lines than any manned ticket counter, especially in the larger stations. To verify their presence in a particular station, check Trenitalia.com, select "In the Region," choose a region, select *Servizi in Stazione*, and look for a dot in the Self-Service column that corresponds to the town/station name.

If you're not purchasing a national ticket and can pay cash, look instead for a blue-

 and-gray Regional ticket vending machine; larger in principal stations, smaller more remote ones. They issue only chilometric tickets (average cost is one to ten Euro), are just as simple to operate, and may keep you from having to stand in line behind all the "tourists" when you're just going from Orvieto to Rome.

> ❋ WORTH NOTING: You can purchase local tickets through a national ticket vending machine, but not vice-versa. You can also buy regional train tickets at an *edicola* or *tabaccaio* in or near the train station (especially in smaller towns where the station ticket window has limited hours).

When using the self-service machines, try to be aware of those in line behind you. They'll often not have much time to spare, so to make them wait while you decide whether to take the Eurostar or InterCity is worse than dawdling in the passing lane on the *autostrada*. If you can spare the time, let anyone in a hurry jump in ahead of you, or look for a machine that only takes credit cards — the line will be shorter there.

ATTENZIONE: If your trip includes a connection, make sure you retrieve one ticket for each leg of your journey from the machine (i.e., one change = two tickets).

Validate Your Ticket

Once you see that your train is indeed in the station, validate your ticket by stamping it in one of the yellow boxes located throughout the station and at track entrances. There is a hefty fine for tickets not validated, and any attempt to claim ignorance as a tourist will earn you a shrug at best. If the train departs and your ticket is not validated, notify the conductor immediately (There's no need to validate a Eurostar ticket because the reservation means it's good only for that specific trip.)

Rail Passes

We simply don't see the point of purchasing rail passes for travel within Italy. To make them cost effective, you have to ride from the Alps to the toe; and they're no longer as convenient as they once were, as reservations and supplements must be purchased in advance and at additional cost for all but regional and IC trains.

The Train Station

Once in the station, look overhead for the big *TRENI IN PARTENZE* (*TRENI IN ARRIVI* for arrivals). The trains will be listed in order by their departure time, and will include ultimate destination (or origination), platform number (*binario*), the type of train, principal intermediate stop(s) (*Ind. Suss.*) and any delay (*Rit*).

> *ATTENZIONE:* Only the train's ultimate destination will be listed on the board. If you're not headed for the last stop a train makes, you can verify your stop using the schedules posted in the glass cases (see The Train Schedule: *Orario* ahead), or on the TrenItalia.com web site beforehand.

The track/platform number (BIN, or *binario*) will be listed on the board only when your train is approaching the station. If the train is late, the intended arrival time should be on the *ARRIVI* board — along with the expected delay in minutes under the column *Rit* for *ritardo*.

Aside from the ticket counters, you'll also find a salon devoted only to train information (*Informazioni Treni*). When you're traveling

PARTENZE				
destinazione	ind. suss.	cat.	ore	bin.
ROMA T.NI	VIA FIRENZE S.M.N.	ES*	14.33	7
VICENZA		REG	14.37	13
ADRIA		REG	14.42	20
UDINE-TRIESTE	VIA CONEGLIANO	REG	14.50	12
GENOVA	VIA MILANO C.LE	IC	14.54	8
TRIESTE	VIA PORTOGRUARO	REG	15.01	4

to locations outside of Italy, have complicated travel plans, or other questions that require more explanation before you make a travel decision, it's best to start in this office. The attendants will speak English and will be able to devote more time than anyone on the platform or at a ticket window.

The Train Schedule: *Orario*

The train schedule for the entire Italian (as well as that of the European) rail system is adjusted a few, pre-established times per year. When travel increases, trains are added schedules are supplemented (in March and in June, for example); when travelers diminish at season's end the schedule is reduced and trains removed (in December).

This current seasonal schedule is available online at the TrenItalia web site; and for a specific location, on posters in pedestal- or wall-mounted glass cases in every train station in Italy. You'll find them inside and out, along walls, and at entrances to and positioned along platforms. They can provide a good deal of supplemental information if you take just a moment to decipher them.

> ❋ **WORTH NOTING:** Your lodging will likely have the current schedule for trains to and from the nearest station.

These posters list, in chronological order, every train due to depart (*Partenze*) or arrive (*Arrivi*) in a 24-hour period from or to that particular destination. Listings include information such as

- the time, and type of train, number and/or name
- class info (1-2), and reservation requirements (R)
- whether there's restaurant, bar, or trolley service
- if bicycles are permitted, if it's wheelchair accessible, or if it has sleeping accomodation
- final destination, arrival time, and every inter-mediate destination and time
- whether the service is guaranteed if there's a strike (*sciopero*)

- and the track/platform number (the big numeral at the far right of each listing

There are some additional notations that may be more difficult, but not impossible, to interpret should you need to. If you have a specific question, there will always be someone nearby willing to help.

The large overhead boards will have the most current information for your train, so always double-check there (see an example at the end of this chapter). These printed schedules can often provide you with the information you need, without your having to stand in line at the information or ticket counter.

Deposito Bagagli: Luggage Drop

Heading to one destination, but interested in visiting another en-route? Leave your luggage at the Baggage Deposit while you're sightseeing, and then reclaim it before continuing on. Cost varies depending on the location — just make sure to verify the opening and closing times before you leave the office, and allow time in case there's a line when you return.

To check the availability at a particular station, go to TrenItalia.com, click In the Region, select the province on the left, then *Servizi in Stazione*, your town/station, and look for a dot in the *Deposito Bagagli* column.

All Aboard

If you haven't already done so, validate your ticket using the yellow machines at the head of the platform. If you have a reservation, locate the carriage number (*carrozza*) and seat number (*sedia*) on your ticket. For example, your ticket may read as follows:

> CORRIDOIO CENTRALE
> NON FUMATORI 2 006 71

The above indicates that the coach has a center aisle (as opposed to compartments), is in second class, car number 6, and seat number is 71.

ATTENZIONE: If you accidentally board a train without a validated ticket (and we've all done it), look for a conductor right away and pay the small fine — or wait for one to find you, and pay the big one.

A first-class will be marked with a large **1** near the coach entry doors, second class with a **2** (the classes will likely be separated by the dining car — when there is one). The individual coach numbers are about half that size, and on the newer trains, will be illuminated, LED displays. If you have any problem, look for a conductor (in the green jacket with FS on the pocket) and show him your ticket.

Board the train only when you've located your assigned (or chosen) coach. Otherwise, you'll be maneuvering the aisles with your luggage, resulting in the inevitable traffic jam when you meet oncoming passengers with their luggage (picture an airplane aisle with less room and more bags)

When you find your assigned *carozza*, board the train and look for your seat number. Depending on the type of train, the seat number may be marked differently, but won't be difficult to locate. Don't be surprised if you find someone in your seat — just show them your ticket and they will move. Or, if there's an empty seat or two nearby, sit there instead. It's far more important to have a reserved seat than to sit in your assigned one.

If you have no reservation, continue down the platform until you spot a car that looks moderately empty, then hop on. To confirm whether a seat is occupied, just point to it and ask, "*Libero?*" (Is this seat free?)

> **WORTH NOTING:** If you're in a coach where pairs of seats face each other, a convenient place to stash a midsized bag is in the space created by the seats that back up to each other.

On Eurostar trains (especially those traveling longer distances) there is luggage storage at one end of each car, which is convenient, quite safe, and will save you from having to haul your bags down the aisle.

On *InterCity* trains, many cars will have compartments (containing six seats each in second class, and four in first) with doors that close, curtains that cover windows, control of overhead lighting and seats that pull forward to meet each other and make a bed. Other cars will have center aisles, and be very similar in comfort and quiet to the Eurostar. In the compartments, the luggage storage is overhead and the capacity is somewhat limited, so if you have lots of bags or they're quite large, you may end up having to leave them in the aisle for others to trip over. Newer cars have extra luggage storage at the end of each car as well as overhead.

> **WORTH NOTING:** If you happen to end up on an train with no place to sit, grab a flip-down seat long the wall of the corridors in the compartment cars, or even in the area between the coaches.

The remaining regional and commuter trains will have more limited luggage space. The overhead storage will hold only smaller bags. Just stash them where you can, and if the train is not too full, feel free to use passenger seats or the space between them.

> **WORTH NOTING:** On Eurostar, *IC* or *IR* trains, you can adjust your seat using a bar or lever located either beneath and at the front, or at the side of each seat. There are no seat adjustments on local *R* trains.

In The Station and at Ticket Counter

binario	track	*sportello*	counter
biglietto	ticket (beel-**yet**-toh)	*viaggio*	travel, voyage
biglietteria	ticket vendor	*vietato*	prohibited
prenotazione	reservation		
stazione	station	**Train Schedules**	
treno	train	*arrivi*	arrivals
		ammessi	admitted
abbonamento	season ticket, subscription	*durata*	duration
acquistare	to buy, acquire	*giornalmente*	daily
agenzia di viaggi	travel agency	*giorni lavorativi,*	
andata e ritorno	round-trip	*giorni feriali*	week days
assistenza clienti	train client information	*giorni festivi*	holidays
attraversare clienti	train client information	*ind. suss.*	intermediate stop
città	city	*orario*	schedule
corsa	course; route	*partenze*	departures
corsa semplice	one-way	*ritardo*	delay
ferrovia	rail station	*si effettua*	in effect (operates)
finestra	window	*sospesa*	suspended
informazioni treni	train information		
lungo percorrenza	long distance		
obbligatorio	obligatory		
rimborso	reimbursement		
solo andata	one-way		
sottopassaggio	underpass		

On the Train

carrozza	car; carriage	*fermarsi*	to stop
corridoio	corridor	*fermata*	(train/bus) stop
libero?	free (not taken)	*questa fermata*	this stop
posto	place	*prossima fermata*	next stop
salire	to get on (train or bus)	*ultima fermata*	last stop
scendere	to get off (train or bus)	*fra due fermate*	2 stops from now
sedia	seat		

. . . you can fling open the windows in your hotel onto the piazza or canal below (and there's no screen, either).

GETTING AROUND: Other Options

Regional Buses

Regional bus lines have large, comfortable, climate-controlled motorcoaches that travel routes on which trains are either unavailable or too cumbersome to be convenient. For example, if you're staying in Florence, the train to Siena is an hour and a half, but there's a regional SITA motorcoach (around the corner from the train station) that arrives in an hour. You can also ride SITA to San Gimignano, Greve, or Radda in Chianti; locations otherwise unreachable from Florence without a car.

SITA lines operate throughout Italy. You can ride these blue buses traveling south from Naples through Sorrento and all along the Amalfi coast without a car. They also operate the Burchiello, a boat that travels from Venice up the river Brenta, excellent for visiting the exquisite Palladian villas located along the banks.

You can get information on destinations and schedules for regional buses from the local TI or APT (see the Tourist Information chapter), and depending on how common traveling by these lines is at your destination, your hotel may be able to give you information as well. Because these are private companies you won't be able to get a ticket in advance (except at their own agencies), but you will be able to buy your ticket on board.

See the Appendix for regional bus lines listing info.

Ferries and Boats

Ferries, or *traghetti*, connect the mainland of Italy with its many islands, from Elba to Sardinia to Sicily and beyond. In the south, many people make hourly day trips from Naples to Capri and Ischia. Travel to Corsica, Sicily, and multiple destinations on the islands of Sardinia and Elba (with or without your car) from the Tuscan ports of Livorno and Piombino, and to Greece from east coast ports, including Venice. There are overnight passages for longer journeys, as well as the high-speed *aliscafo* or hydrofoil, which is both faster and significantly more expensive. Italian *traghetti* are not luxury liners, but are very comfortable with many conveniences aboard, such as bars, lounges, deck chairs, etc.

If you're planning to travel by ferry in the summer, you'll need to reserve your tickets at least one month in advance. If you're already in Italy, the best place to check your options for an impromptu trip will be with your hotel, the Tourist Information office (for nearby destinations), or a local travel agency, where'll they'll speak plenty of English, explain all your chioces, and book tickets as well.

See the Appendix for a list of major ferry companies and their destinations.

Air Travel within Italy

There are a variety of low-cost airlines that offer economical fares both within Italy and across the European continent. The Italian company MyAir, for example, and RyanAir (out of Dublin), offer excellent fares to select destinations. There are quite a few others, each one originating in a particular European country and serving specific, if diverse destinations. The fares can range from reasonable to unbelievably low (€14 from Paris to Milan), and there are one-way fares with no penalty. These airlines may use the principal airports that the major carriers do, or alternate airports located some distance from metropolitan areas (although these airports frequently offer convenient transport options to city centers, train stations, and other airports). These airlines may fly in and out of smaller cities you may not normally consider: Pisa, as opposed to Milan or Florence, for instance.

If you choose to take advantage of one of the amazing fares, do make sure you understand exactly where the airports are located. If you're looking to zip down to Palermo from points north instead of putting in the required number of hours on a train or ferry, these airlines certainly make it possible to do so.

> *ATTENZIONE:* When investigating these fares, make sure when you purchase that you also have a confirmed seat on the flight you're booking. Some fares do not include reservations and are good only if seats are available. In addition, read the fine print for applicable taxes, operations, and service fees that can cause a significant increase in the final fare amount.

We've listed web sites for some of the most popular intra-Europe airlines in the Appendix. Review the fares, then check with a local travel agent to compare other schedules and fares they may have available.

Lost Luggage: *Bagagli Smarriti*

If your luggage doesn't arrive when you do (this happens most often when you have a connecting flight with a short layover at a large airport), don't despair — just follow the same procedure you would at home. Go immediately to the Lost Luggage counter, or *Bagagli Smarriti*. They'll speak English, and will have you fill out a form with pertinent information about your bag and where you're staying. Your bag will be brought to you by courier when it arrives, which is very often on the next flight from the connecting airport. Do get their phone number, and give them any numbers where you might be reached: hotel, cell phone, etc.

> ❋ WORTH NOTING: A courier will bring your bag or bags to you wherever you are, even if you'll be staying somewhere other than the city where you arrived.

Vocabolario

Bus (*autobus*)

capolinea	head of the line
corsa	route; course
in attesa	will arrive within...
fermata	bus stop
linea	line
previsione	expection of arrival
pullman	tour bus, motor coach
suburbana	suburban line
urbana	urban, metro line

Ferry (*traghetto*)

approdo	approach
aliscafo	hydrofoil
costa, costiera	coast, coastline
mare	sea
mare grosso	heavy seas
mare mosso	calm seas

Airplane (*aereo*)

aeroporto	airport
campagnia aerea	airline company
cabina	cabin
volo	flight

General

a bordo	on board
acquistare	purchase
agenzia di viaggi	travel agency
arrivo	arrival
andata e ritorno	round-trip
corsa semplice	one-way
solo andata	one-way
biglietto	ticket (beel-**yet**-toh)
biglietteria	ticket vendor
bagagli smarriti	lost luggage
città	city
collegamento	connection
conferma	confirmation
destinazione	destination
disponibile	available
linea	line
minuti	minutes
ore	hours
orario	schedule, timetable
origine	beginning of route or line
pagare	pay
partenza	departure
passeggeri	passengers
porto	port, door
prenotazione	reservation
punto di vendita	where to buy tickets
sedia	seat
servizio	service
sicurezza	safety
sospesa	suspended
tariffa	fare, price
viaggio	trip, voyage

Local Bus Service

If you live in a metropolitan area and are already used to bus travel, you'll have little trouble adapting to Italian mass transit. City buses in Italy are used as much as the trains, with routes that are generally reliable and convenient. After taking time upon your arrival to familiarize yourself with a few principal lines, you'll be zipping around town effortlessly and economically, and feeling much more like an Italian than a tourist. Each town will have its own individual bus system along with specific options for types of tickets, but there will be enough similarities among them that it should pose no problem to use public transportation in any town.

There will always be dedicated offices offering bus tickets and route information at train stations and airports, and also at various locations around the cities themselves (ask at the Tourist Information office). In some cities such as Bologna, bus tickets are dispensed by machines on the street. You also can buy bus tickets at newsstands and at the *tabaccaio*, but there they may not have bus maps or route information.

Bus and transit tickets may be purchased in a variety of forms. Tickets may be good for one ride or for a period of time (a day, week, or longer). There may be a ticket that's good for a certain number of trips, sold as a pass or a book of tickets. For instance, a single, one-way, €1 ticket in Rome is good for 75 minutes of bus, metro, and tram travel, while a single ticket in Florence still costs €1, but is only good for 60 minutes, due to the city's smaller size. In Florence you may buy a *carnet*, or four tickets in one for about €4, while in Venice you may buy passes good for a period of time: 1 day, 3 days, or a week, for example; likewise for the ferries in the lake region. Because these options will vary from city to city and are constantly evolving, make sure to review current options to get what will best suit your needs.

> ❧ WORTH NOTING: There are always public transit offerings from the airports to main train stations. They're usually comfortable, acclimatized motorcoaches, with luggage space below, and economical way to arrive in the city center. Ask at the airport or train station bus counter.

In Bologna, for example, the bus system has been enhanced to allow you to buy a single ticket on board for €1. We hope other systems will follow, but for now assume that you must buy your ticket *before* you board the bus.

Validate Your Ticket

The buses in Italy run on the honor system. You don't have to show your ticket to anyone as you board, but *it is your responsibility to carry a valid ticket anytime you're riding the bus*. A valid ticket is one that has been stamped, and whose period of validity, whether for an hour, a week, or a month, has not expired. There are officials who will board intermittently (more frequently than you'd think) and then ask to see everyone's ticket. If you don't have one, or it has not been stamped (*timbrato*), or the time has expired, it could end up being a very expensive ride.

In contrast to the train, you'll always stamp your ticket after you board the bus using the machines provided there at the front and back. For single tickets, you'll stamp them when you board. If you've bought a ticket that's good for three days, for example, you'll only stamp it the first time

you board, and it will then be valid for the next seventy-two hours.

ATTENZIONE: The exceptions are the water-buses, or *vaporetti*, in Venice. There's no machine to validate your ticket on board, so as with trains, you'll stamp your ticket *before* you board at the machines available at each stop.

Buses in Italy generally have three entries, are boarded from the front or rear, and are exited from the center doors. Move toward the center as your stop is coming up, and if you need to get by others to get off, simply say *"Permesso."* Other passengers will understand that you're disembarking and let you pass, but when you can, avoid embarking at the door where people are getting off, and vice-versa.

ATTENZIONE: Don't be seduced into thinking that because no one else is stamping their ticket, you don't have to. It's very likely the other passengers have tickets that are good for the day, week or month, which means that if the official boards to check, they will have valid tickets, and you will pay the fine.

In the Metro

You may not ever venture onto the subway system in Milan or Rome — the centers of cities are quite navigable by alternative means, including your feet. But, to cover a significant distance you may decide to use the subway, so allow yourself plenty of time to become oriented to their layout and to review ticket options.

The systems are large and almost always bustling, and can be confusing, mainly because they'll be new to you. Allowing an extra ten minutes to make sure you get your tickets, locate the train going in the right direction, and find the correct exit at your destination can make all the difference. Maps of metro lines are available at any city transit office (though they can become scarce toward the end of the season).

Taxis and Limousines

Taxis are convenient but pricey in tourist centers, so when you choose them, make sure you'll get your money's worth. When you can share the ride, when the weather is intolerable, when there are time constraints, or to get to the airport with lots of luggage, a taxi is a logical choice. Under normal circumstances though, trains, regional buses, local buses, and your feet will do nicely.

Throughout Italy, there are many limo services available that can be engaged to transfer groups and for charter activities. They are not inexpensive, but if you have a large group they definitely help smooth connections. You can locate these through travel services and agents in the U.S., in Italy, and on the Web.

On Foot

It's important to understand that many addresses in historical centers may have originated a century or more ago. Many have come and gone; others have been squeezed in between the originals, with the end result often being quite confusing to the uninitiated. It will be a great help if you can somehow get a dot on your map before you launch out to find a particular location.

For in-town offices and personal residences, you may not have a unit number, only a street address. Once you arrive at the building itself, look for the name you've been given on the panel by the door.

Press the button next to the name. You'll either be buzzed in immediately, or hear a voice ask *Chi è?* (Who is it?) Tell them, and enter when you hear the click of the lock.

> ❋ WORTH NOTING: There is no consistent system for odd and even addresses from one town to another; there can even be duplicate addresses on both sides of the same street. In Florence, 35R (*rosso,* or red) is officially a business address, but a black 35 is a residence. If you arrive at an address and it's not what you expect, see if there's another across the street.

Vocabolario

Buying tickets and getting information

autobus	bus
abbonamento	season ticket, subscription
acquistare	purchase
andata e ritorno	round-trip
solo andata	one-way
biglietto	ticket (beel-**yet**-toh)
biglietto ordinario	good for one ride
biglietto giornaliario	good for one day
biglietteria	ticket vendor
coinvalidare	to validate
orario	schedule
premere, premete	press (button)
punto di vendita	where to buy tickets
tariffa	fare
timbrare	to stamp
tasto	button
capolinea	head of the line
corsa	course; route
fermata	bus stop
linea	line
suburbana	suburban
urbana	urban, metro
viaggio	trip

At the bus stop...

ammessi	admitted (animals, bikes)
arriva	arrives
dura	it lasts...
giornalmente	daily
giorni lavorativi, feriali	weekdays
festivo	holiday
in attesa	waiting for...
in ritardo	delayed
parte	departs
si effettua	in effect (operates)
si ferma	it stops
sospesa	suspended

On The Bus

posto	place
libero?	free? (not taken)
scendere	get off
salire	get on
sedia	seat
fermata	(train/bus) stop
fra due fermate	in 2 stops
questa fermata	this stop
prossima fermata	next stop
ultima fermata	last stop
permesso	permission (to pass)

. . . architectural curves and flourishes outnumber straight lines
about 10,000 to 1, and the saints and archangels are
continually blessing you from above.

KEEPING IN TOUCH

Phoning in Italy: He Who Calls, Pays.

Italian Telephone Numbers

Phone numbers in Italy are composed of a **prefix**, followed by the individual **phone number**. Unlike North American phone numbers, neither contains a fixed number of digits. The prefix may be from two to four numbers in length, and for land lines, will always begin with 0. This prefix is not officially an area code, but does in fact indicate where the phone is located (the prefix for Rome is 06, Firenze is 055, Orvieto is 0763). All cell-phone prefixes are three digits and begin with a 3. The entire number will be from five to eight digits, although cell phone numbers will always be ten digits, just like we're used to.

> ❧ WORTH NOTING: Always dial both the prefix *and* the phone number — from anywhere in Italy to anywhere in Italy — even if you're in the same building as the person you're calling.

Call Costs

There is normally a per-call charge for every Italian phone call made. Whether calling from a land line, cell, or pay phone; the cost will consist of an initial charge for connection (*scatto alla risposta*), followed by a per-minute charge. The per-minute charge is more expensive during business hours, but drops significantly in the evening and on weekends (especially Sunday).

Since the advent of Internet service providers offering phone service as well, we've seen the introduction of bulk-calling packages for land lines, and land cell combinations; as a traveler, you not likely have access to many of those, however.

Keep in mind that when phoning in Italy,

- the caller always pays for the call, whether from a land line, pay phone or cell phone;
- it can cost more to call a cell phone from a land line than from another cell phone;
- phone calls from hotel rooms can be extremely expensive, even using a phone card;
- it can cost more to make a call during the day than in the evening or on Sunday.

Making International Calls

When making any international call (from Italy to any other country, or vice-versa), the number you dial will be composed of three parts:

- an international dialing code
- the destination country code
- the individual phone number.

The **international dialing code** tells the local system that you'll be dialing another country instead of the one you're in. This code can vary from one country to another, as noted below. So, to begin your international call, first dial:

011	from the U.S., or
00	from Italy and Europe

You'll then dial the destination **country code** (just as they are here, with no additional zeros):

1	country code, U.S.
39	country code, Italy

The entire number you'll dial will look like this:

00 1	area code, number	(Italy - U.S.)
011 39	prefix and number	(U.S. - Italy)

From the U.S., to call 06 52 62 455 in Rome, dial

  011 39   06 52 62 455

From Italy, to reach 512 480 5115 in Austin, dial

  00 1   512 480 5115.

If you're using a phone card, there may be an access number and pin to enter first, but these are the formats for the phone numbers themselves when you're calling from one country to another.

Fail-safe Cell Dialing +

You may have noticed a + used in international phone number notation. This plus sign represents each individual country's international dialing code, and your cell will recognize it as such. You can utilize this feature on ANY cell phone, in, from, or to ANY country, using ANY service provider, to always reach the party you intend, by dialing

  +   country code   phone nbr (w area code)

Adopt this habit prior to traveling for storing and dialing all your numbers, and you'll avoid having to make any adjustments once abroad.

> ☀ WORTH NOTING: To dial **+**, hold down the 0 (zero) key, or press the asterisk * twice. Otherwise, consult your cell instruction manual or service provider.

Using Phone Cards

You can buy two types of phone cards at your local *tabaccaio*. The first may be used in pay phones, and is best for making domestic calls; the other can be used from any phone, best for making international calls to a specific country.

The Italian phone card (*scheda telefonica*) is convenient for making domestic calls from any public phone, and is sold in two denominations (€5 and €10). It's quite handy if you're using pay phones regularly, because all phones accept them, and there's no need to worry about having change.

> ❋ **WORTH NOTING:** Before you use the phone card for the first time, tear off the corner at the perforation — otherwise it won't slide into the phone properly.

To use the *scheda*, choose your language, then slide the card into the phone as indicated. The phone will display the initial credit available, and you'll be able to view the remaining credit as you talk. Don't forget to take the card with you when you're done.

The second type of calling card is much more economical for phoning home. Ask the *tabaccaio* for an *international* phone card (most likely available in tourist centers). They'll ask what country you'll be calling, as there are various cards for different parts of the world, issued in denominations of €5 to €50. **Europa** is a popular brand, as is the Sisal **Edicard**, issued as a slip of paper with all pertinent information. (You can also credit your Italian SIM card and buy lottery tickets at Sisal affiliate bars and *tabaccai*. Look for the green and white **SISAL** logo.)

> **ATTENZIONE:** Calling North America with the *scheda telefonica* is extremely expensive — you can easily use the entire card for one call without being able to finish your conversation. Use these cards for making domestic calls only.

The international phone card is used differently from the *scheda* that you slide into the phone slot. Instead, dial the toll-free access number, select English, and when prompted, enter the pin number (provided with the card), followed by the destination phone number. You can use it from pay phones and private phones alike (and from 5s too, though you'll get fewer minutes total).

> **ATTENZIONE:** *Make sure* you use the correct toll-free access number. It must be the Italian number, not an American toll-free number.

Finally, before your departure, you can also arrange for an international phone card from an American telecom company. When doing your research, ask:

- if there is an initial charge for connecting,
- how much you'll pay per minute for a call;
- how to access customer assistance from abroad

ATTENZIONE: You may or may not pay an extra charge to use your phone cards from your lodging — be sure you ask at check in.

Pay Phones

Stainless steel touch-tone pay phones have now all but replaced the old pulse-dial phones (the orange ones) which made it impossible to operate any touch-tone menus to check voice messages, for example. However, as cell phones become the norm, pay phones themselves are becoming more and more scarce. You'll find them at stations, internet points, and in phone banks, but they're quickly disappearing from many other locations.

Land phones, such as those you may find in an apartment you're renting, have had touch tone dialing for some time, so you'll have no problem there.

What's that noise?

The sound you'll hear while the phone is "ringing" is different from what we normally hear, alternating pulse tones instead of one that imitates a ring. A faster beep-beep is a busy signal. One that's faster still actually means the call is still being attempted, so just hold on a few seconds — it will probably go though.

Online in Italy

You'll find plenty of Internet access points scattered throughout Italy, and their number is increasing almost daily. There are everything from dedicated salons and cafes with banks of wired computers to single computers tucked away in bars, hotels and even retail stores. Your lodging may have a common access point available for guests, but Wi-Fi is also becoming increasingly common, as it's much easier to install than a wired network. Your hotel should also be able to point you to a nearby Internet cafe (and because things are changing so rapidly, you may even discover another on the way there). The price can range from €3 per hour.

> ✦ **WORTH NOTING:** Italian keyboards are slightly different than U.S. keyboards, as are British keyboards, etc. To create the @ on an Italian keyboard, hold the *Alt Gr* key to the right of the space bar, then press the @ key, located just right of the *L*.

Most every Internet service provider has Web-based e-mail access. Even if you normally use an e-mail client such as Outlook Express on your home computer, you should also be able to retrieve your mail using a Web browser such as Firefox. Before you go, check with your Internet Service Provider for instructions on how to access your mail using a Web browser, or use a no-cost Web mail service such as mail2web.com. (Any mail you do not delete using these services during your travels will be available to access as you normally do once you return home.)

Taking Your Laptop

If you're planning to take your laptop along and have network capability (you have a network card or an Apple portable), you may hook into the network at many Internet points at no additional charge. Wireless capability is rapidly becoming common at hotels and other lodging, though less so at actual Internet points.

You may also connect using a modem if you have a telephone available for your use. Cords and connections are identical to ours, so no adapter is necessary in all but the most remote instances (otherwise, phone wallplug adapters are available at Italian electronic supply stores.)

Your laptop's electric power adapter should already be equipped with dual-voltage capability, but verify this using the information on the power adapter itself (it will read 110-220v), or in the instruction manual. You'll need a **plug adapter**, though, in order to be able to plug into the wall; in Italy these are available at most any electrical supply store for about €2.

> ✦ WORTH NOTING: Your modem will likely not recognize the Italian pulse dial tones. Make sure you instruct your computer **not to wait for a dial tone** when attempting dial-up access.

If you can do it safely, stash your laptop inside your carry-on rather than in its own bag. Otherwise, a laptop case will substitute either for your personal or carry-on bag on your flight; and as such becomes yet another item which must be managed in transit from one location to another.

Many companies sell a variety of leaner cases, bags, protective sleeves and other creations which protect your laptop, yet allow you to pack it safely along with other items in a personal carry-on. This has the added benefit of not announcing to every passerby that you're carrying a laptop, allowing you to stay a bit more at ease en route.

Internet and the Computer

Many technology-associated words will be English ones, and most of the assistants you'll encounter at Internet points will be English-speakers, too.

| @ | *Alt Gr* key (right of the space bar), and |
| @ | (right of the *L* key) |

computer	computer
punto d'Internet	Internet point
sala d'Internet	Internet salon

chiocciola	the @ sign (literally, a spiral)
collegarsi	connect
in rete	on the net
guasto	not working
non arriva	doesn't load (e-mail, Web page)
punto	dot (i.e., *punto* com)
pagina Web	Web page
scaricare	to download
schermo	the screen
stampare	to print
stampa	the printer

Phoning

telefono	telephone
numero	number
chiamata	phone call
segreteria telefonica	voice mail
messaggio	message
parlare	to talk

fare un numero	dial a number
rispondere	to answer
riagganciare	to hang up (handset)
un attimo solo	wait one moment
scadenza	expiration
scaduta	expired (card value)

operatore	operator
rete fissa	land line; fixed line
cellulare,	
telefonino (colloq.)	cell phone
informazione	information
numero verde	toll-free number

| *scheda telefonica* | phone card |
| *scheda internazionale* | intern'l phone card |

English terms:

e-mail, Web, Internet, broadband, ADSL, fax, online, software, hardware, at (@), computer, and more.

. . . you are never surprised to pass a nun, monk, or priest
    in full, traditional habits and robes — with laptop in tow.

Where there's a bank, there's a Bancomat

Currency Exchange

There are two expenses involved in currency exchange: the *rate of exchange* (how many Euros you'll be given for your dollars), and the *service fee* you're charged for each transaction. It's good to be aware of both of these amounts when choosing your mode of exchange.

As we noted in *Planning Your Adventure*, you'll be relying on the *Bancomat* as your primary cash source because it's the most convenient, and offers the best exchange rate with the lowest service fees (verify these with your bank). A *Bancomat* is never far away, and so allows you to travel with less cash and more peace of mind. The cash machines are quite easy to operate: once you choose your language they function just as they do at home.

It often makes sense to get the maximum amount of cash allowed each time you do a cash withdrawal, to keep to a minimum the number of trips to the *Bancomat*. Stash the big bills in your money belt if you prefer, keep handy cash in your wallet, and you're set.

On the remote chance that a cash machine keeps your card, go inside the bank (if it's open) and ask if it can be returned to you. If the bank is closed, and you're not able to return, they'll normally send the card back immediately to the issuing bank (which is why it's best to bring more than one card that will operate a cash machine).

If you prefer to exchange currency by other means, banks will give you the next best rate. Banking hours are a bit inconvenient (8:30 A.M. – 1:30 P.M. and 3:30 – 4:30 P.M.) and their operation is not terribly efficient, so don't plan on this being a quick stop.

Whenever you have a choice, avoid the *Cambio* counters in train stations or anywhere else; the exchange rate is rarely favorable and the fees are quite high.

The Euro

The elegantly designed Euro currency has been maintaining an advantage against the dollar in recent years, which makes it even more important not to treat it like "play money." Some of the most noticeable differences in the Euro and the dollar are:

- ← there are a €1 and €2 coins, but there's no €1 bill — the lowest-valued note is €5;

- there are 2c and 20c Euro coins, but no "quarters;"
- the size of both bills and coins gets larger as their value increases.

※ WORTH NOTING: The €1 and €2 coins are easy to locate among the others because they're larger, and two-toned: the €1 coins are gold-colored in the center and silver-colored on the outside; the €2 is larger and the colors are reversed. All other coins become smaller according to their value, are solid gold-colored; under 10c the tiny coins are in copper.

Credit cards

Cash will always be king in Italy, at least for the foreseeable future. Although use of credit cards has certainly become more widespread in recent years, it should never be a surprise that any given establishment accepts only cash. Hotels will often request a credit card to hold your reservation, but will always prefer currency for payment. And anytime you pay with a credit card, be aware that you'll always be paying more — not only for card fees, but to compensate for the nearly 20 percent tax that must be paid on reported income.

※ WORTH NOTING: If you pay cash, you can at least request a small discount (*sconto*) at markets and establishments frequented by tourists; but never with a credit card.

ATTENZIONE: Do be aware that merchants often will not accept credit cards in smaller towns less frequented by travelers. Plan always to pay in cash; if you find you have the option, use a credit card if you prefer.

Avoiding Trouble

A friend arrived for a visit recently with a typical horror story: a woman traveling on the same overnight train to Venice had been robbed of 2000 Euros, wasn't that awful? Certainly, but *why* in heaven's name was this woman, who was traveling alone, carrying €2000 in cash — and on a night train, knowing she'd be sleeping for long periods? Couldn't she have traveled with a smaller amount of cash, waiting until she arrived in Venice station to obtain more from the station ATM, or even a bank?

True stories and urban myths circulate continually about unconscious tourists being relieved of cash and belongings while traveling through Italy and Europe. The operative word here is *unconscious*.

There are highly-conscious thieves (of various nationalities) who will happily abscond of your valuables if you present them with the opportunity. This is not out of spite or because they want to punish you, but more likely because either it's how they've been raised to support themselves (gypsies, or *zingari*), or it's the only means of support they have available to them at the moment.

Like Florida, Italy is surrounded by water on three sides, and boasts thousands of miles of shoreline. And then there's the island of Sicily, just a stone's throw from northern Africa. When things heat up in other countries, and inhabitants there decide to seek a better life elsewhere (which is what you and I might do), Italy is a logical choice, even as an intermediate destination. It's quite handy, and monitoring all the modes for illegal entry is practically impossible. Once in the country however, these *extracomunitari* are unable to work legally, so they either sell stuff on the streets, or steal yours (they assume you can easily get more). This is strictly a survival mechanism. It's important to understand though, that unlike the stereotypical "mugger" in the U.S., they have *no desire to do you any physical harm*, whether with a gun or any

other type of weapon. This would not feed their families — they only want your stuff.

They know how much money tourists carry, how they carry it, and when and how they are most easily distracted. The most likely places where problems may occur are crowded buses and Venice vaporetto, train stations, metro stations, airports, and popular tourist routes such as along the Arno River in Florence, the Calle della Rasse leading from San Zaccaria in Venice, or around the Spanish Steps in Rome. Anywhere there is a famous, congested tourist destination, there are pickpockets looking for easy targets.

Our personal theory: *make the pickpocket pick somebody else.* Put yourself in the pickpocket's place: what clues would indicate a person might have more stuff than they could ever use? To avoid issuing an unconscious invitation, follow these guidelines — particularly when sightseeing, or in transit:

⤺ **Leave your expensive jewelry at home.**

Any pickpocket would assume that if you've got a big rock on your hand, you've got a wad of cash in your wallet. Have you seen any other bejeweled travelers about today, Italian or otherwise? For ultimate safety, if you must travel with your favorite baubles, stash them when in transit.

☙ Dress comfortably, even stylishly if you like, but not ostentatiously.

You'll impress no one but the potential pickpocket. Save the most stunning apparel for the gala when you're not carrying any valuables or lots of cash. (Again, this applies principally when en route and in crowded environments.)

☙ Don't put all your cash in one place.

This advice made more sense when the *Lira* was Italy's currency and there were many more bills involved. Still, it's something to keep in mind if you've just taken a hefty withdrawal from an ATM. Put some in your wallet, and larger bills in your money belt or in a secret pocket in a carry-on or other bag. Then, on the off-chance you do become a target, you'll suffer only an inconvenience instead of a devastating blow.

☙ Do not put anything valuable in fanny packs, back-slung purses or anything else that hangs behind you — they just proclaim, "Yoo-hoo, here's my stuff."

Instead, carry a bag or purse that hangs comfortably and securely under your upper arm or across the front of your body. These do not have to be specially designed travelers' bags, but can be any bag that is roomy, light, and hangs naturally under your arm when on your shoulder. That way, it stays in a secure position without your having to think about it constantly, and it doesn't shout to the potential pickpocket "Hey, I'm a tourist and my expensive camera is *right in here.*"

☙ Never leave anything valuable unattended.

Never, ever. When you sit outside at a crowded cafe in a popular *piazza*, keep your bag in front of you, as opposed to hanging casually on the back of your chair or on the ground underneath you out of sight.

On the train, we have no problem storing our bags in the racks provided at the end of any Eurostar car, or asking a passenger to keep an eye on our stuff while we

go to the restroom or dining car (they understand as well as you do the importance of keeping an eye out). We stay more aware of our luggage on local and regional trains though, where there's more opportunity for getting off and on.

← It's best not to leave anything of value in your car, in or out of sight.

One reason cars cost more to rent in Italy is that vandalism is a real problem throughout the country, and any insurance included in your rental coverage is quite expensive. We've rented cars in Italy off and on for years, and have never had any problem — but we have heard of people who have. To reduce the chances of what could be an extremely unpleasant situation, make it a habit to remove anything of value from your car before leaving it in a parking lot, attended or not.

We've lived and traveled in Italy for years, independently and with others, with no problems whatsoever. Only once did we get in trouble at the airport, leaving a purse and luggage on a cart behind us while chatting with the agent at the ticket counter. When we turned around, the purse had disappeared with not a soul in sight. Avoidable? Absolutely. If we'd only followed our own advice.

Lastly:

← Be alert, not paranoid.

If you follow these guidelines and are neither frantic or oblivious, you'll stay at ease during your travels and will have no sad stories to recount on your return home.

Vocabolario

Bancomat	ATM, cash machine	*soldi, denaro*	money
annulla	clear, annull	*sconto*	discount
cancella	cancel	*spiccioli*	coins, change (colloq.)
esegui	proceed (enter)	*travel check*	Traveler's Checks
fuori servizio	out of service		
		banca	bank
carta di credito	credit card	*cambio*	exchange, exchange rate
caparra	deposit, down payment	*ufficio di cambio*	money exchange office
cauzione	security deposit	*sportello*	counter
contante	cash		
dollari	dollars	*bagaglio*	bag
Euro	Euro	*borsa*	purse
moneta	coins, currency, money	*portafoglio*	wallet
il resto	change		

. . . \$5 will buy you either a gallon of gas or a liter of very nice wine. (We prefer the wine.)

EATING and DRINKING

or, The Most Important Thing is to Eat Well.

There is a saying in Italy: Only tourists eat bad food. We get tired, distracted, and succumb to the invitation of the nice *cammeriere* outside a handy restaurant, or plop down in front of the nearest thing that looks even remotely digestible, pay big bucks and are sorely disappointed. Where would this most likely happen? In places where there are the most tourists, of course, or at least enough to support a bad restaurant.

No Italian would ever, *ever*, think of consuming anything that is not as good as they could've prepared themselves (or, at least *la Mamma*). The artisan values that are inherent in Italian culture extend right into the kitchen. Meals and the sharing of them with friends and family are something to be celebrated. So it follows that something you prize so highly, you attempt to do as well as you can. Italians *demand* quality in the meals they are served (otherwise, what's the point?). That's also why, once outside the tourist centers, you rarely have to worry about the quality of the restaurant. If it's in business, you'll likely get a lovely meal.

The quality of any Italian meal begins with quality ingredients: it's crucial to use only the best and freshest available. That's why it's not unusual to hear an Italian inquire about the specifics of the meat or fish or pasta dish he's about to order, or to hear a server, completely nonplussed, respond to his inquiry in detail. He fully understands the importance of assuring his customer of the quality of the food he's about to serve.

Types of Eateries

Knowing how important food is to Italy, you might guess they have words other than restaurant for the various types of eateries and what they serve. These are the traditional definitions, although they are no longer adhered to as strictly as they once were:

bar Not a bar as we know it, but a cafe where you'll find brioche and pastries for breakfast, *panini* and *tramezzini* (sandwiches) for lunch (a *tavola calda* means they have hot, prepared dishes as well), and everything from *caffè* to cognac to sip while you sit, converse and watch the world go by — for as long as you like. A bar opens early, stays open all day and will usually close at about 7:30 or 8 P.M.

osteria   Once a tavern that offered beds for the night (it's where we get the word *hostel*), this public house will normally have a modest and cozy atmosphere, serve wine by the glass, and have a limited but tasty menu of meat and cheeses, pasta dishes or regional specialties, often with an extensive wine selection.

trattoria   Where friends meet for a great meal and a good chat. Traditionally family-owned and operated, your local trattoria can be like a second home. It's a warm, familiar place, and the owners, wait staff, and longtime regulars are often a type of extended family. They'll take great pride in offering you a solution to all the problems of your day in the form of a hearty meal and a menu sufficient for ordering anything from a *primo* to four or more courses, often specializing in the owner's version of the regional cuisine. (In a trattoria, you may have to ask for a second glass if you want both water and wine...we don't know why.)

ristorante   In a *ristorante*, you'll get two glasses without even having to ask. They're a bit more formal, elegant, and expensive, and may have a more extensive or specialized menu. If you're in a tourist center, make sure you have an Italian recommendation (other than your hotel) before dropping into just any *ristorante*.

There's also the *enoteca*, or wine bar. Here they'll offer sales and tasting of fine wines, occasionally with food. (In Venice, they're called *bacari* and are more casual places where locals socialize over a glass of wine to discuss the events of the day.)

Some *trattorie* are also *pizzerie*, and there are storefronts offering *pizza d'asporto* (to go) and *pizza all'taglio* (by the slice); but *vi prego*, please enjoy yours sitting down.

> ※ WORTH NOTING: At a bar, you'll typically pay the server or cashier (at the *cassa*) after you've ordered and eaten. At certain bars (in train stations or at *autostrada* stops, for example) you'll make your selections first, pay the cashier, and then take your receipt to the counter, where you'll be served the items you ordered.

For any eatery other than a bar, the menu will frequently be posted outside for your review — if it isn't, don't be shy about asking to see it. Don't sit down though, until you've committed to eating there.

Aperitivo: The Cocktail, Italian Style

As a rule, Italians are not big drinkers. How can this be, with all the fine wine they produce? There's a saying in Italy: *Never eat without drinking, never drink without eating.* Italians are masters at designing cocktails, wines, and liqueurs as perfect accompaniments to everything from *antipasti* to entrees, or to promote scintillating conversation, but rarely is drinking a recreational activity in and of itself.

As a result, the Italian cocktail remains a true *aperitivo*, designed to whet the appetite and induce *un po' di allegria* (a bit of cheer) into the dinner conversation. To try this custom, choose an inviting bar and ask the bartender or server for an *aperitivo*, specifying any of the following characteristics according to your preferences:

dolce, o secco	sweet, or dry
alcolico, non alcolico	alcoholic, non-alcoholic
forte, o meno forte	strong, or less strong

If you ask for something alcoholic, dry and strong, you might get a *Negroni* (and you'll only want one of these). If you'd like something alcoholic but less strong and a little sweet, you might be offered an *Aperol Spritz*. Dry, alcoholic and less strong might introduce you to a *campari soda*. We're not sure if the non-alcoholic creations have names, but they'll be delightful. There are specialties of the house, or *aperitivo della casa*, and of individual cities, such as the Venetian *Bellini*, that are always a good bet. Be adventurous — if it's not to your liking, your gin and tonic will be waiting in the wings as a fail-safe.

Whether you order a *prosecco* or an *acqua minerale con limone*, you may always toast your companions with either *Salute* ("To your health"), or more commonly, *Cin cin!*

> ❧ WORTH NOTING: *Vino alla mescita* is wine by the glass, and originates from the *mescita* — in many a Renaissance home, a small, street-level window opening to the wine cellar from which a glass of the family's own wine was sold to passersby.

The Italian Meal

You won't eat this way at every meal — not even locals do, day in and day out — but plan to set aside certain occasions to eat as Italians do when they're celebrating: consciously, energetically and joyously. If you do it right, it will bring new meaning to the word *nourished*.

Antipasto This is an appetizer, we just adapted our word from the French "appetite" instead. Often a cold sampling of regional vegetable or meat specialties; in Venice or along the Amalfi coast where fish is the thing, you may be served a variety of fresh, cold seafood, or *insalata di mare*.

Primo The first course is pasta, gnocchi, risotto or soup (*minestra*). Split it with someone if you must, but include it if you can.

Secondo The main course can be meat, fish, or a *frittata* (an omelette), which you may order with *contorni* (vegetables or other accompaniment), and follow with a salad, or *insalata*. Salads here function much more as a palate-cleanser than an appetizer — which makes some sense, doesn't it?

Dolci Save room for dessert — again, split if you must, but do indulge!

Ordering

It's common to order mineral water with your meal, but you'll be asked to specify "with or without gas." There are naturally fizzy spring waters as well as carbonated ones, so if you have a preference you can inquire about that as well. Order a liter of water for two to four people, and more as you need it.

If you are not a wine connoisseur, or just looking to accompany a pizza or *panino*, feel confident in ordering the house wine by the full, half- or quarter-liter. They'll be young, served *sfuso* (in a carafe), locally produced, quite palatable, and cost a fraction of any bottled wine.

Servers in Italy are accustomed to Italians who know exactly what they want and how they want it. They can sometimes be of little help when asked for suggestions about what's good, but will be more than willing to answer any questions you might have about the menu itself. You may also ask about the regional specialties, if you're not familiar with what they might be.

Don't ever worry that you're the only vegetarian they've ever seen, or the only person who must avoid dairy, gluten, salt, and more. Feel perfectly comfortable describing your dietary requirements — most likely your server will be able to suggest an alternative. (Practice the Italian vocabulary and phrases for communicating your dietetic needs.)

When your meal arrives, don't forget to offer the customary salute to your companions: *Buon Appetito* (which effectively translates to "Stop talking and eat!").

> ❊ WORTH NOTING: Perhaps you're not a connoisseur, but whether you have only a mildly developed wine palate, or are simply curious about sampling wines from producers never found outside of Italy, we'd encourage you to further explore the Italian *eno terreno* with some fine, bottled wine; especially when it's paired with an equally fine meal. Branch out from your Chianti or Brunello comfort zone, and search out wines from grapes and regions you're less familiar with. If you're not confident to select on your own, choose a *ristorante* or *enoteca* known for its wine list, then ask for suggestions. It doesn't have to be a costly experiment — and you may even end up searching for a bottle or two to take back with you.

The *Digestivo*

Just as the *aperitivo* whets the appetite, the *digestivo* can aid in helping that wonderful meal digest properly. This is a very small amount of what is usually a fairly potent liqueur: *Amaro*, brandy, *sambuca*, *limoncello* or the ever-popular *grappa*. *Grappa* is a wonderful, if quite robust after-dinner drink — distilled from the skins and stems of grapes — but make sure it's a good one. There's simply nothing worse than bad whiskey, or bad *grappa*.

> ❊ WORTH NOTING: Unless you're very tired and very desperate, best to avoid the *Menu Turistico*. It will save you little, and you'll be served the most generic food on the menu, aimed at the least discriminating palate (reread the opening motto of this chapter).

La Pizza

Napoli is the accepted home of the original pizza, but its mouth-watering offspring can fortunately be had throughout the country. A delicious pizza *fatta in casa* (homemade) is a quicker, more economical, but still highly-satisfying alternative to the traditional Italian meal. The pizza crust is often cracker-thin and very tasty, and the ingredients are fresh, from cheeses to meats, vegetables, exotic sauces and more. To be truly authentic, it will be baked in a wood-fired oven.

Because the crust is thinner and the ingredients so fresh and flavorful, they're used sparingly and as a result make for a lighter, more savory pizza. And since they're not exceptionally large, it's not unusual to order one pizza for each person at the table. Of course this will not be the case when ordering a *pizza Siciliana*, or Sicilian style, which will be more of a true "pizza pie," with a thick, tasty crust and lots of sauce, cheese and toppings.

Coperto, Servizio, Tax and Tipping

A *coperto* is what you're charged for having service at your table, as opposed to standing up at a bar. The cost will vary with the class of eatery, but it's almost inevitable in the tourist meccas, though rarer in smaller towns.

Tax on your meal is in fact almost 20 percent, but it's included in the total price of the meal as opposed to being itemized on your receipt (the proprietors will pay it themselves according to their proceeds)

The *servizio*, or service charge, is intended for the servers, although they may not necessarily receive it (or all of it). So should we tip?

Being a server in Italy is a profession and a full-time job. As a result, servers are paid a living wage with benefits, and so do not survive on tips. Still, we use these guidelines: although it's not expected in small towns, 5 percent is a good tip for good service. In tourist centers however, the work is grueling and thankless: we leave 10 percent unless the service is awful. Use your judgement, but be aware that leaving more can appear arrogant — even insulting.

ATTENZIONE: If there's a particular eatery you want to sample, confirm its closing days, and make a reservation — especially in a popular tourist destination (everyone else knows of this restaurant, too). If you're eating before 7 P.M., though, you and the other two tables of Americans should have no problem.

It's not coffee...it's *caffè*

When our friends Gabriella and Roberto were visiting us from Italy (their first time in the U.S.), we ordered *espresso* from a food-court vendor in the mall, who served it to us in little paper cups. Gabriella looked at us, looked at the cup, turned to Roberto and said, "If you served someone coffee in Italy this way they'd throw it in your face."

She wasn't being critical — just truthful. *Caffè* (which is *espresso*) is routinely served in a ceramic cup and saucer anywhere you order it in Italy, and is just one of those things that *matters* — there are some areas in life where one simply must not compromise.

If you can get past the very American more-is-always-better syndrome, Italian coffee can be some of the most satisfying you'll ever have. (Now admit it, don't you get tired of drinking lukewarm coffee after three sips?) Don't worry, if *espresso* is not your cup of tea, you'll have no trouble getting American coffee, or at least something that resembles it.

> ❧ WORTH NOTING: The server is not ignoring you, but leaving you to bask in the afterglow of a wonderful meal. Therefore, the bill will never appear on your table until you've asked for it. (Have you had your *dolce, caffè,* or *digestivo*?)

Gel-*ahhhhh*-to

The good news is, Italian *gelato* (ice cream) does not have more calories than American ice cream. The bad news is, it's everywhere, and it's *delizioso*.

Of course, the best gelato is *fatto in casa*. If you're seeking only the best, inquire before investing time and calories. If you're on a gelato mission, when you stop in the TI on your arrival (see Tourist Information), ask them to dot your map with the best *gelaterie* in town.

Many gelato stores will offer not only ice cream, but sorbet, soy ice cream and even frozen yogurt. Some *gelaterie* have only a few flavors, yet others offer an astounding array of creative flavors and colors from *tiramisù* to *zabaione* (see the end of the *Vocabolario* in this chapter for a list of common gelato flavors). It's easy to be adventurous: just select an old favorite and combine it with one or more unknown new ones.

In a *gelateria*, you'll first decide how you'd like your gelato, either in a cup (*coppa*) or cone (*cono*), and then what size you'd like. There'll be some examples on display so if you prefer you can point to your selections. You'll typically pay first, then take your receipt to the gelato counter to select your flavors; otherwise they'll serve your order first and you'll pay afterward.

Buon appetito!

Vocabolario

Types of eateries:

bar	cafe (drinks and sandwiches)
tavola calda	cafe with hot, prepared food
self-service	cafeteria
osteria	simple menu, good wine.
trattoria	family-owned, local dishes
ristorante	restaurant (more formal)

The meal:

mangiare	to eat
colazione	breakfast
pranzo	lunch
cena	dinner
spuntino	a snack

Reserving and inquiring:

prenotazione	reservation
Vorrei prenotare...	I'd like to reserve...
un tavolo	a table
stasera	this evening
domani sera	tomorrow evening
due persone	two people
(tre, quattro)	(three, four)
È possibile avere...	Is it possible to have...
qualcosa di veloce?	something quick?
qualcosa senza carne?	without meat?
qualcosa di leggero?	something light?
solamente un primo?	pasta only?
specialità della casa	the house specialty?

Getting your server's attention:

Signore...	Sir...
Signora, Signorina...	M'am, Miss...
Mi scusi...	Excuse me...

At your table...

menù	menu
piatto	plate
tovagliolo	napkin
forchetta	fork
coltello	knife
cucchiaio	spoon
bottiglia	bottle
tazza	cup
bicchiere	glass

What your server might say:

Allora.	Now.
Che cosa desidera?	What do you desire?
Cosa volete?	What would you like?
Cosa prendete?	What would you have?
Avete deciso?	Have you decided?
Certo	Certainly.
Poi?	And then?

Ancora?	More for you?
Lo scaldo?	Shall I heat it up?
Basta così?	Will that be all?
Com'è?	How is it?
Tutto a posto?	Everything alright?

What you might say:

Cos'è...	What is...
Ho fame.	I'm hungry.
Ho sete.	I'm thirsty.
Io prendo...	I'll have...
Potrei...	Could I...
Vorrei...	I would like...
questo	this
quello	that
poco	a little
molto	a lot
uguale	the same
un altro	another
Per favore	Please
Grazie	Thank you
Prego	You're welcome

Special concerns:

diabete	diabetes
allergico	allergic
vegetariano	vegetarian

va bene il pesce	fish O.K.
niente...	no...
alcool	alcohol
caffeina	caffeine
glutine	gluten
latte	milk, dairy
olio	oil
sale	salt
zucchero	sugar

Drinks and drinking:

bere	to drink
sete	thirst
bevande, bibite	beverages, drinks
un bicchiere di...	a glass of...
acqua	
minerale	bottled water
frizzante or	carbonated or
con gas	naturally fizzy
dal rubinetto	tap water
caffè	espresso (with an s)
caffè latte	steamed milk with *caffè*
latte	steamed milk only
caffè machiato	stained with steamed foam
cappuccino	steamed milk and foam, nutmeg and cinnamon
con panna	with steamed cream

caffè **corretto**	with a shot of liquor	*vino*	wine
caffè **americano**	with hot water added	*della* **casa**	house wine
cioccolata **cal**da	hot chocolate...literally.	*bianco*	white wine
tè	tea	*rosso*	red wine
tè **freddo**	cold tea	*rosato*	rose wine
al limone	lemon flavored	*sfuso*	by the carafe
alla **pesca**	peach flavored	*alla* **mescita**	by the glass
tè **caldo**	hot tea		
succo	juice, or	*degustazione*	wine tasting
spremuta	fresh (squeezed) juice	*vendemmia*	grape harvest
d'arancia	orange	Meals and food:	
di ananas	pineapple	*mangiare*	to eat
di albicocca	apricot	*fame*	hunger
di mela	apple		
di pompelmo	grapefruit	*sale*	salt
aperitivo	cocktail	*pepe*	pepper
digestivo	after-dinner	*zucchero*	sugar
		Antipasti	appetizers
alcohol content:		*Primo*	1st course:
alcoolico	alcoholic	*minestra*	pasta soup
forte	strong	*pasta*	pasta
leggero	light	*polenta*	corn meal pasta
corposo	full-bodied (wine)	*risotto*	rice
generoso	very strong (wine)	*zuppa*	soup
birra	beer	*Secondo*	entree
alla **spina**	on tap	*carne*	meat

frittata	omelette	*fragole*	strawberry
manzo	beef	*limone*	lemon
bistecca	steak	*mele*	apple
pollo	chicken	*mirtillo*	blueberry
pesce	fish	*lampone*	raspberry
prosciutto	ham	*pesca*	peach
uova	egg	*pompelmo*	grapefuit

Contorni

verdure	vegetables	*contorni*	veg. accompaniment
asparagi	asparagus	*formaggio*	cheese
carciofi	artichokes	*pane*	bread
fagioli	beans	*dolci*	sweets, desserts
funghi	mushrooms		
insalata, lattuga	salad, lettuce	**How it's prepared...**	
patate	potatoes	*alla griglia*	grilled
pomodori	tomatoes	*arrosto*	roasted
rucola	arugula	*bollito*	boiled
spinaci	spinach	*cotto*	cooked
zucchine	zucchini	*crudo*	raw
		fumicato	smoked
frutta		*fritto*	fried
albicocca	apricot	*misto*	mixed
ananas	pineapple	*scaldato*	heated
anguria, cocomero	watermelon	*soffriggere*	fry lightly
arancia	orange	*stagionato*	aged
ciliege	cherries	*a vapore*	steamed

La Pizza:

These have a tomato sauce and mozzerella:

acciughe	anchovies
asparagi	asparagus
caprese	fresh tomato and basil
capricciosa	mushroom, artichoke, olive
diavola	with spicy sausage
funghi	muchrooms
margherita	tomato, garlic, olive oil
napoletana	capers, anchovies
quattro formaggi	four cheeses
quattro stagioni	four ingredients
rucola	arugula

These have no tomato sauce:

burro e salvia	sage and butter
pizza bianca	olive oil and rosemary
pizza al taglio	by the slice
pizza d'asporto	to go

How is it?

Buono	good
Molto buono	very good
Buonissimo!	the best!
caldo	hot
freddo	cold
delizioso	delicious

The bill...

il coperto	the cover
il conto	the bill
la mancia	the tip
il servizio	the service charge
il resto	your change
ricevuto	receipt
scontrino	register receipt

Gelato

coppa	cup
cono	cone

Some common flavors:

amarena	black cherry
arachidi	peanuts
bacio	(kiss) Rocky Road
cioccolato	chocolate
crema	vanilla
gianduia	chocolate shavings
mandorle	almonds
nocciola	hazelnut
noce di cocco	coconut
panna	cream
soia	soy
stracciatella	cream and chocolate
zabaione (zabayone)	meringue and liqueur

...it's 1 p.m., and the store you're interested in will be open again at 3:30 p.m. Maybe.

Lo SHOPPING

Although super-duper, one-stop shopping is slowly invading Italian suburbs, traditional Italian-style shopping involves visiting small, specialized shops selling meats, fresh bread, fish, produce, milk products, etc., all from local producers. These shops are often centered around a nearby *campo* or *piazza* that's within walking distance of home, and allowing the cook to pick up whatever's needed for the upcoming meal without having to get in a car.

As a tourist in a hotel, you may not be doing any shopping for meals (although if you've chosen to stay in an apartment, you may). But there are plenty of other shops that will interest you, whether or not you'll be preparing lunch. Here's an overview of some of the various types of shops you'll see, and what they sell.

The *Tabaccaio*: Your One-Stop Sundry Shop

The tobacconist, or *tabaccaio*, is so called because it's the only shop licensed to sell tobacco products. Whether or not you ever need any of them, you can seek out a *tabaccaio* for any of the following:

- ✦ phone cards (local and international)
- ✦ local bus and metro tickets

- ✦ stamps, postcards, envelopes
- ✦ photo supplies
- ✦ facial tissues
- ✦ bottled water, mints and gum
- ✦ local train tickets (if in or near a station)
- ✦ something to write on
- ✦ something to write with
- ✦ and, of course, cigarettes.

It's worthwhile to check at the *tabaccaio* first for whatever you're seeking. If they don't have it, they'll tell you where you can get it.

You can spot a tobacconist by looking for the big, white **T** on a blue or black background. It may be an individual shop, but bars may be tobacconists as well. Just keep an eye out for the T, and learn the phrase, *Dov'è un tabaccaio qui vicino?* ("Where is a tobacco shop nearby?")

The Newsstand: *l'Edicola*

Just like the tobacconist, the Italian newsstand typically has resources beyond what the name implies. Newsstands proliferate in train stations, airports, and city centers. You can purchase local bus tickets, regional train tickets (if it's in the station or nearby), and they'll also sell the complete seasonal train schedule in booklet form (called *InTreno*). They'll sell local and regional maps, as well as guidebooks to the city and region in English and other languages.

In larger town and tourist centers, newsstands sometimes carry English-language publications, such as European versions of the *New York Times* and *Wall Street Journal*, and British dailies such as *The Times* and the *International Herald Tribune*, among others.

The Bookstore: the *Libreria*

If you're in Milan, Florence, Bologna or Rome and you've forgotten your *Blue Guide* or *Time Out*, find the local *Feltrinelli International*, Italy's largest bookseller. The "International" part of the name indicates that the publications they stock are in a host of languages other than Italian, including English. You'll find extensive collections of city, province, and regional, as well as country maps. There are English/Italian dictionaries of every size and subject (looking for a cooking dictionary?), and an extensive selection of travel guides for any location in the country, from *Frommer's* to *Rick Steves* to *Time Out* and more (just in case you need something else to carry around).

If you're interested, ask the attendant at the TI (see the chapter on Tourist Information) to mark the Feltrinelli, Rizzoli or other international bookstore on your map.

Food Stores

The Grocery: *Alimentari*

The *alimentari* has a little bit of everything, from staples such as coffee and pasta, to deli meats, olives and cheeses, and even prepared foods such as pasta sauces and marinated vegetables, with maybe a little fresh bread thrown in for good measure. They'll likely have drinks including water, milk, and a selection of local wines. In other words, it's a wonderful place to stop to prepare a picnic lunch before starting off to explore the countryside.

> *ATTENZIONE*: It's customary to have the vendor handle produce for you. If you do handle it yourself, look for disposable plastic gloves nearby to use instead of your bare hands.

Individual Food Stores

You can always spot a *supermercato*, or supermarket, which will be similar to those we have at home (only not quite as super). This is the place to find most anything you'd look for in any supermarket anywhere.

Otherwise, these are the specialty shops:

Frutta e Verdura	fruits and vegetables	Fresh produce
Macelleria	butcher shop	Fresh meats and regional specialties
Latteria	dairy	Milk, yogurt, cheese products, eggs
Enoteca	wine shop	Wine and associated; wine tasting.
Pasticceria	pastries	Cakes and desserts
Panificio	bakery	Fresh baked goods
Pescheria	fish	Fresh fish & seafood
Gelateria	ice cream	One of the main reasons we come here.

Other Types of Stores

The Pharmacy: la *Farmacia*

The Italian pharmacy will always be identified by a large, red or green neon cross. Pharmacies are open normal business hours and usually close during the lunch break.

Pharmacies in Italy don't carry the broad array of merchandise available in U.S. pharmacies. They do carry medicines and homeopathic drugs, health-related items such as orthopedic products and ear plugs, and perhaps some cosmetics and toiletries. If you should begin to come down with a cold or sore throat, don't be afraid to step into a *farmacia* and describe your symptoms: the pharmacist will be happy to suggest a remedy for minor ailments.

> ❧ **WORTH NOTING:** There is always one pharmacy in town that is available for the emergency dispensation of medicines, day or night. It may be the same pharmacy always, or it may rotate, in which case its name will be posted on any pharmacy door. If it's quite late, you may have to ring for the pharmacist to let him know you're in need of service.

Stores for Clothing and Hair

Abbigliamento	Clothing, men's or women's
Biancheria	Lingerie
Grandi magazzini	Department store
Parrucchiere	Hair Stylist
Barbiere	Barber

Miscellaneous

Cartoleria	Stationery
Ferramenta	Hardware
Elettrodomestici	Electronic supply (adaptor plugs)
Mobili	Furniture
Ottico	Optician and eyeglasses
Foto Ottica	Photographic supplies
Lavanderia	Laundry (self-serve or drop off)
Lavasecco	Dry cleaners (pay at drop off)

Local Markets

In every town, there are local markets that occur weekly on a certain day, sometimes two days, sometimes every day. They are great fun, and there'll be an abundance of everything from food to clothing to housewares to...well, just about anything you can name. Depending on the size of the market, there may be a new merchandise section and even a used merchandise section (a recent concept in Italy, where people normally use up everything completely before tossing it aside). There are also antique markets, which occur a bit less frequently, but can offer wonderful browsing and some unique and rare finds.

Check at your hotel, or the local TI or APT (Tourist Information office) for when, where and what types of markets will be in town when you are.

The Cash Discount: *Sconto*

Each time you purchase something in Italy, the proprietor will be obliged to pay the government a value-added tax, or *IVA* (*Imposta Aggiunto su Valore*): almost 20 percent of the purchase price. In fact, you'll often notice items advertised with the phrase *IVA inclusa* (tax included) or *più IVA*, which means they'll add on the 20 percent at the cash register (suddenly, 7 percent doesn't seem so bad).

Sometimes — and you'll have to be a bit intuitive about this — you may receive up to a 10 percent discount if you pay cash. This gives you a small discount and allows the proprietor to retain more of the purchase proceeds. Whether this is an option will vary greatly depending on the location, the store policy, whether it's a local market or an upscale store, and on subjective factors up to and including the mood of the proprietor and how gracious you yourself have been up to that point. We wouldn't expect it, but it never hurts to ask.

The VAT Refund

As a foreigner you're entitled to a complete IVA, or VAT tax refund *if* you spend more than €155 in any one store. If you're planning on buying some portion of Italy to take home with you (and you will be tempted), familiarize yourself with the following steps in order to receive your rebate. The on-your-own process is a bit labor intensive, but will work if you have no other option:

First, *let the merchant know you intend to apply for an IVA refund* on your return. They should provide you with a receipt or invoice (*fattura*) for the goods purchased. Ask them, *per favore*, to itemize the list of purchases along with the amount of tax paid. The invoice will also include the phrase *"Esente IVA ai sensi delle legge 38 quartiere,"* which states that your purchase is IVA exempt.

At the airport (allowing plenty of time), *take the receipts with the merchandise to the customs office*, either in this airport, or from wherever you're departing the EU. There they will validate (stamp) your receipts.

When you arrive home, *mail the validated invoices to each individual store* (within 90 days), and they'll either send you the refund, or issue a credit against the card you used when you made your purchase. This procedure can take anywhere from two weeks to two months; but as they say, everything in Italy happens eventually.

There is a an easier way to obtain the VAT refund, however. There are a variety of companies (and their store affiliates) that allow you to collect your refund in any airport on your departure from the EU, and sometimes even beforehand in local city offices. These orgainzations have done a superb job of simplifying the VAT tax-refund process, making it practically pain-free. Follow these steps to avail yourself of one of them.

↞ While shopping, keep an eye out for prominent stickers indicating that a store is a tax-refund company affiliate.

↞ When you make your purchase, ask the sales clerk for a Tax Free Check (Global Refund) or other appropriate form. They collaborate closely with these organizations and will be well aware of what you'll need.

✦ Allow plenty of time in the airport, and take the forms, receipts, merchandise, and your passport to the customs office (prior to airport security check) when departing Italy, or last EU country of departure. The customs officials will validate your form.

✦ Go immediately to the associated cash refund office (post-airport security) where you'll have several options for reimbursement. (There may be the possiblity complete this step in the U.S., but it can be more complicated). For locations of the cash refund offices in EU airports and additional information, check the associated tax refund company web sites, or locate the information on the associated documentation you're provided.

> ❀ WORTH NOTING: If a store ships goods directly to your residence in the U.S., the purchase once again should be IVA exempt, so make sure your receipt also indicates you paid no tax.

Depending on the tax-refund company, there may also be the possiblity of obtaining your refund in Italy, in cash, from a local office (normally in principal centers like Rome or Venice). Ask the store affiliate if they're aware of this option, and if so, where the offices are located.

One final shopping note: most proprietors view their stores as a second home, and as such take great pride in them. We were visiting a friend who owns a small store in Venice when two travelers entered the store. "*Buongiorno,*" greeted the owner, to which the customers did not respond. They toured the small shop briefly and exited. "This is something I don't understand," commented my friend. "It's as if someone comes into your house without even saying hello or goodbye. Certainly I don't expect everyone who enters to purchase something, but not to give the courtesy of a hello or thank you...what are they thinking?"

We have no idea what nationality these travelers were, and perhaps common courtesy is not always so important to every shop owner. But it may enrich your own experience a bit more to acknowledge whoever is there to assist you whether or not you eventually make a purchase.

> ❀ WORTH NOTING: For information on restrictions and duties for bringing items back into the U.S. from abroad, see the *Know Before You Go! Online Brochure* at the U.S. Customs and Border Patrol web site, www.cbp.gov/xp/cgov/travel/.

Vocabolario

Stores and shops:

bottega	shop or workshop
negozio	store
grandi magazzini	department store
mercato	flea market
supermercato	supermarket
alimentari	grocery store
cartoleria	stationery and asso.
farmacia	pharmacy
edicola	newsstand
lavanderia	laundry
lavasecco	dry cleaners
libreria	bookstore
pasticceria	pastry shop
panificio	bakery
tabaccaio	tabacconist
saldi	sale
in offerta	special offer

What shopkeepers say:

Mi dica.	Tell me (May I help you?)
Pronto?	Ready (to order, to go)?
Cosa volete?	What would you like?
Certo.	Certainly, of course.
Com'è?	How is it?
Come va?	How's it going?
Basta così?	Will that be all?
Ecco!	Here (it is, you are)!
Tutto a posto?	Everything alright?

Things you'll buy:

cartoline	postcards
penna	pen
matita	pencil
pellicola	film
fazzoletti	tissues
francobolli	stamps

...to wear:

camicia	shirt, blouse
cappotto	overcoat
gonna	skirt
giacca	jacket
giubbotto	sport overcoat
maglia	knit shirt
maglietta	t-shirt, vest
pantaloni	pants, slacks
vestito	dress
cintura	belt
cravatta	tie
cappello	hat

		Making your purchase:	
guanti	gloves	IVA	(ee-vah) VAT tax
sciarpa	scarf	IVA inclusa	tax included
scarpe	shoes	più IVA	plus tax
gioielli	jewelry		
orecchini	earrings	fattura	invoice
anello	ring	ricevuto	receipt
catena	necklace	scontrino	cash register receipt

Trying things on:

misura	size	Quanto costa?	How much is it?
taglia	cut, size	Non sono sicuro.	I'm not sure.
Posso provare?	Can I try it?	Va bene.	O.K.
		Lo prendo.	I'll take it.
Troppo...	Too...	pagare	to pay
grande	big	C'è uno sconto	Is there a discount
piccolo	small	per contante?	for cash?
lungo	long	Carte di credito?	credit cards?
corto	short	Travel Check?	Traveler's Checks?
stretto	tight	Potrei...	Could I...
		Vorrei...	I would like...
gratis	free	Vorrei comprare...	I would like to buy...
caro	expensive	È possibile spedirlo?	Is it possible to ship it?
rotto	broken		
È bellissimo!	It's beautiful!		
Mi piace.	I like it.		

. . . you can walk, leisurely and at midnight, down some of the
most beautiful streets in the world with no fear for your safety.

SHIPPING and THE POST

Posteltaliane: The Italian Post Office

The ongoing evolution of the Italian post office has resulted in services that are more efficient, better-organized — and more diverse than you might think. They include telegrams, fax and telex transmissions, wire transfers, the sale of telephone cards, lottery tickets, train and bus tickets, and prepaid VIAcards for the autostrada; and there is always one or more public phones. A Postamat works just like a Bancomat to retrieve cash, and the bright yellow and blue color scheme makes postal stores easy to spot.

Because stamps and postcards are also available at the tabaccaio, you may not need to go into a post office at all...unless you get tired of lugging all that stuff you brought (or bought) and decide to ship some of it home.

ATTENZIONE: In the post office, the counters with **blue €** signage are designated for financial transactions (Prodotti BancoPosta), while the **lime green** signs with **envelope** icons indicate postal services (Prodotti Postali).

Your hotel can point you to the nearest post office, which are often noted on city maps. Post Offices are normally open from 8:15 A.M. through 6 or 7 P.M. without a pausa, some even on Saturday. Smaller branches may close earlier, however, so it's best to check.

International Shipping Options

For **letters and postcards** there's Posta Prioritaria, or priority mail (although there's no non-priority option). Stamps can be purchased from the post office or a tabbacaio (when they're not sold out). Just let them know the destination and they'll provide you the correct postage.

For **express shipments outside Europe**, Posteltaliane offers Paccocelere Internazionale for parcels weighing up to 30kg. (This replaced EMS, or International Express Parcel; still available to only a few small countries.) Paccocelere costs range from €20 to €200 for packages weighing up to 45 pounds. The service is reliable, and shipments are trackable, arrive in three to four days, and cost less than equivalent shipments by private shippers like UPS, FedEx, DHL, or the national company, Bartolini.

If you have a **large package** and speed is not critical, there is *Pacco Ordinario,* which can travel either via air or surface (buy ship to the U.S.). The service is still reliable, and costs far less than an express shipment, although delivery will take anywhere from ten days to two months and will not include real-time tracking.

❀ **WORTH NOTING:** When you have a choice, ship the stuff you brought, and take the stuff you bought home with you. This will simplify packaging requirements and reduce the likelihood of customs delays. When shipping post, lighter and bigger is often less expensive than smaller and heavier.

PosteItaliane sells boxes for packaging in a variety of sizes, priced at €1 and up. They do not sell packing material, however, so you'll have to provide that (from a *tabaccaio or cartoleria*).

Here are comparisons for relative price and shipping times among the three options for an average-sized, **5kg** (just over 10 lbs.) parcel:

Ordinario, surface	€26,60	< 30kg	2-3 mos.
Ordinario, air	€52,03	< 30kg	10-14 days
Paccocelere Inter.	€72,60	< 30kg	3 days
EMS	€98,15	< 20kg	2 - 5 days

NOTE: These estimates include no customs and duties for which you may be liable. There is always the possibility of Customs delays that can contribute significantly to shipping time.

Private Shipping Services

The three most common international shipping services available in Italy are DHL, FedEx and UPS. There are shipping locations throughout Italy, but your best approach will be to call their central office (where they will speak English) and research rates, arrange for pickup or find a location near you. See the Appendix for a list of phone numbers and Web addresses.

The following are sample rates for comparison to ship a 10 lb. (approximately 5 kg), one-foot square package. Size, weight, and destination will affect the price. If applicable, duties and taxes will be assessed en route and due on receipt.

DHL	2-day	$139
FedEx	Priority	$129
	Economy	$107
UPS	Express	$103
	Expedited	$98

Stores and businesses will usually offer one or more ways to ship your purchases, but this service may or may not include an additional labor charge.

Customs and Duties

On arrival from abroad, packages are forwarded by the postal service to U.S. Customs for examination. Customs will examine and then return them, and they'll in turn be forwarded to your local post office for delivery. If duties have been assessed, they will be due when you receive the package.

Even though shipping time for airmail is quicker and costs more, unpredictable delays can still occur in the custom process. Private, express shipping companies (Fedex, etc.) have agreements designed to expedite the Customs process, so if there's nothing irregular, your shipment will not be delayed there. You'll still be responsible for additional duties assessed according to contents of the shipment.

ATTENZIONE: To avoid unnecessary customs' delays, complete all shipment forms as completely and accurately as possible. The *Posteitaliane* official should be able to give you whatever assistance you need in filling them out, but cannot predict eventual duties, as these are assessed by U.S. Customs.

ufficio postale	post office	*lettera*	letter
accettazione	acceptance	*pacco*	package
all'estero	abroad	*paccocelere*	priority mail w/receipt)
cassetta delle lettere	mail box	*pacco ordinario*	surface shipping, no receipt
corriere	courier	*posta prioritaria*	air, no receipt
cartolina	postcard	*posta raccomandata*	air < 2kg with receipt
EMS	int. express mail	*posta assicurata*	insured; special packing requirements
francobolli	stamps	*prodotti postali*	stamps, etc.
per gli Stati Uniti	to the U.S.	*scatola*	box
imballaggio	packing material	*via aerea*	airmail
scatola	box		

Dovequando

(www.poste.it/online/dovequando/) is the online service (in Italian) that allows you to track the progress of you shipment.

. . . you can linger in the piazza at your favorite cafe and people-watch the day away — without anyone asking repeatedly if you "need anything else?"

TOURIST INFORMATION: *i*

English Spoken Here

The TI Office

Once you arrive at your destination, make sure you stop at the local Tourist Information office, or TI (also referred to as the APT, or the *Agenzia di Promozione Turistica* and even IAT, *Informazione ed Acoglienza Turistica*). Where tourism is well established, it will be an excellent information resource, whether your stay is a day or a month. Although the heavily-toured sites are better organized, adhere more often to posted **business** hours, and have more extensive information available than remote or lesser-known destinations, a trip to the TI is never a waste of time. In addition, you'll often find the highest concentration of people who speak and understand English.

You'll be given maps and complete information on current offerings, events, exhibitions, and excursions, and depending on the location, you'll sometimes be able to buy tickets and make reservations, thus avoiding lines for museums, concerts, and other venues. You can often get a list of Internet points and their locations, book tour guides or perhaps pick up self-guided walking tours. They'll even have local train and bus schedules.

It's always a good idea to make a list of the questions you have before you go into the TI: it's easy to get distracted and there may be a line, and you don't want to forget to ask the most important thing you came there to ask.

> ❧ **WORTH NOTING:** While you're at the TI office, ask for their phone number. And, if you think you'll need to know something in advance for a town other than the one you're in, get that number as well.

If you intend to visit someplace specific, make sure you get opening and closing times for that site (or a list of all opening and closing times). If you don't know much about the area, tell the attendant how much time you have and ask what must not be missed. You can also get recommendations for good places to eat, and the day(s) and location of the weekly market. If you intend to ship anything home, have the attendant mark your map with the locations of the post office or express shipping locations.

There will be TI offices at arrival points and in the heart of the historic centers. Your hotel should be able to give you the hours and point it out on your map. The italic *i* may appear on a brown, yellow or other background but will normally be easy to spot (just make sure it is the official one and not a private tour company doing a good imitation).

Consider visiting museums and other popular sites late in the day when the lines will be shorter and the museums less crowded (most tourists want an early start, and so all line up bright and early; and the schoolchildren's tours will also be in the morning). During high season, many of the most popular sites will be open later into the evening, offering you the possibility of an afternoon *riposino*, and allowing you to visit them a bit more refreshed and at ease.

> ✹ WORTH NOTING: Check to see if there are combination tickets available to state- and civic-owned museums and sites. Review what's included in these offerings to see if they'll suit your itinerary.

Local Tour Guides and Private Tours

Official tour guides in Italy are licensed, have a strong academic background, and have passed an extensive set of exams covering the architectural, artistic, and cultural history of the specific region for which they are licensed. Prices for these guides vary depending on the region and city, but can normally be hired at the APT or TI office. They're usually quite good at what they do, and certainly know their stuff, but can sometimes be somewhat regimented, as they have to cover a certain amount of material in the appointed time.

> *ATTENZIONE:* Saturdays are the most crowded days for popular destinations, with Friday and Sunday not far behind. This is primarily when visitors come only for the day and depart in the evening. You may want to choose these days for more unusual activities or day trips that take you away from the centers. In any case, many destinations will generally be calmer in the evening.

Companies and nonprofit organizations also offer private tours, and sometimes have more creative itineraries that vary widely in content and price. They can have a more relaxed atmosphere while being informative as well. Information on private companies is available through the TI, guidebooks, chat forums, and sometimes your hotel, but should be booked in advance whenever possible.

Tourist Information office checklist:
- Local tour guides, private tour companies
- Concert tickets
- Museum tickets and reservations
- Options for combination tickets
- Maps
- Must-see recommendations
- Current exhibitions and events
- Laundromats: self-service, drop-off or dry-clean
- Internet point locations
- Train and regional bus schedules
- Convenient travel agencies
- Phone numbers for other TI locations
- Market days and locations
- Closing day(s), or afternoon
- Traffic and parking restrictions
- Post office and express shipping locations
- Parking restrictions and recommendations
- Eating recommendations
- Best gelato
- Best pizza
- Special shopping recommendations
- Bank and *Bancomat* locations
- Dates and times for any upcoming strikes

No *Vocabolario* in this chapter — your English will do fine.

...all at once, you hear someone whistling, or singing,

   alone or with others, seemingly for no reason whatsoever.

Then, of course, you realize it's YOU.

APPENDIX A - Z

Airline Companies: Intra-Europe
Airport Web Sites
Assistance and Emergency Phone Numbers
Bus and Metro Companies: Regional
Bus and Metro Companies: Urban
Car Rental Companies
Cell Phone Rental
Conversions/Comparisons
Currency Exchange Rate
Customs Information
Embassies and Consulates (U.S.)
Ferry Companies
Guidebooks and Online Travel Resources
Holidays and Annual Events

Internet Points (chains)
Internet Service Providers (Italian)
Language Instruction
Maps & Driving
Money
Passport Information
Recommended Films
Recommended Reading
Shipping Services
Tax (VAT) Refunds
Time, Date and Number Formats
Train/Rail Pass Fare Comparisons
Train Schedules & Ticketing
Travel Insurance
Travel Time and Cost Estimates

Be sure to download our free companion publication **Planning Your Adventure**,
available at **italyinstructions.com**

APPENDIX A - Z

Airline Companies: Intra-Europe

Air Dolomiti	Verona/Paris,Brussels, Munich, Frankfurt; Venice/Naples	www.airdolomiti.it
BMI	Heathrow/Venice	www.flybmi.com
Easyjet	Stanstead/Orly/Milan	www.easyjet.com
EuropebyAir	Flightpass	www.Europebyair.com
Meridiana	Florence, London, more	meridiana.it
MyAir	Europe and beyond	www.myair.com
RyanAir	Italy from London Stanstead, Brussels, Frankfurt; Paris/Milan	www.ryanair.com
VirginExpress	Brussels/Rome	virgin-express.com

Airport Web Sites

Aeroporto di Firenze (FLR)	www.aeroporto.firenze.it
Milan Airports	Malpensa (MPX) and Linate (LIN) www.sea-aeroportimilano.it/eng/
Malpensa Express	Malpensa by train to Cadorna station www.ferrovienord.it/webmxp/ing/
Malpensa Shuttle	Malpensa to Milano Centrale or Linate www.malpensashuttle.it
Napoli Capodichino (NAP)	www.gesac.it/en/index.html
Palermo International (PMO)	www.gesap.it
Pisa International Galileo Galilei	www.pisa-airport.com
Roma Fiumicino (FCO)	www.adr.it
Venezia Marco Polo (VCE)	www.veniceairport.com
World Airport Guide	worldairportguide.com

Assistance and Emergency Phone Numbers

Assistance
- 12 Directory Assistance, national (English or Italian)
- 176 Directory Assistance, European (English or Italian)
- 1790 Directory Assistance, beyond Europe
- 170 International Operator, free English Dir. Assistance

Emergency
- 112 Police
- 113 Emergency
- 115 Fire
- 118 Ambulance
- 116 Emergency Road Service
(free tows to visitors with foreign license plates or a car rented at the Rome or Milan airports.)

Bus and Metro Companies - Regional

ANAC, Rome	06 4482 0531	
Autostradale, Milan	02 801 161	
Lazzi, Florence	1668 56 010	www.lazzi.it
SITA, Florence	055 214 721	www.sita-on-line.it
Eurolines, London	+44 020 7730 8235	

Bus and Metro Companies - Urban

Metro Info		metropla.net
Firenze: ATAF	800 424 500	ataf.net
Milano: ATM	800 808 181	atm-mi.it
Roma: ATAC	800 424 500	atac.roma.it
Venezia: ACTV	041 27 22 111	actv.it
Veneto: ATVO	0421 383 671	atvo.it

Car Rental Companies See also Alamo, Avis, Budget, Dollar, Hertz

AutoEurope	800 223 5555	autoEurope.com
	00 800 223 55555 toll-free from Italy	
Europebycar	800 223 1516	www.Europebycar.com
Kemwel (U.S.)	877 820 0668	www.kemwel.com
RenaultUSA	800 221 1052	www.renaultusa.com

Cell Phone Rental

PRE-TRAVEL

AutoEurope	800 223 5555	autoEurope.com
CellHire	800 287 3020	cellhire.com
CellularAbroad	800 287 3020	cellularabroad.com
PlanetOmni	800 858 4289	planetomni.com
Telestial	858 274 2686 (US tel)	telestial.com

IN ITALY

Tim	www.tim.it
Vodafone	www.vodafone.it
Wind	www.wind.it

Conversions/ Comparisons

TEMPERATURE:

Celcius	Fahrenheit	Celcius	Fahrenheit
0°	32°	22°	72°
10°	50°	28°	82°
16°	60°	35°	95°

LIQUID VOLUME:

1 liter	=	1.04 quarts	=	.26 gallons
1 meter	=	3.28 feet	=	1.09 yards
10 kilometers			=	6.2 miles

WEIGHT:

100 grams	or	1 etto	=	3.8 ounces
1/2 kgs	or	500 grams	=	1.1 lbs
1 kgs	or	1000 grams	=	2.2 lbs
10 kgs			=	22 lbs
100 kgs			=	220 lbs

Currency Conversion Rates   www.oanda.com, www.xe.com

Customs Information www.customs.ustreas.gov/xp/cgov/travel/

Embassies and Consolates - U.S.   www.usembassy.it

Florence	055 266 951
Milan	02 290 351
Naples	081 583 8111
Rome	06 46 741

Ferry Companies (*Traghetti*)

Ferries Online		www.ferries.online
Traghetti Online		www.traghetti.com
Adriatica	Balkans, Greece	www.adriatica.it
Caremar	Capri, Ischia; Ponza	www.caremar.it
Corsica Ferries	Corsica	www.corsicaferries.com
Enermar	Sardinia	www.enermar.it
Moby Lines	Sardinia, Corsica, Elba	mobylines.com
Sardinia Ferries	Sardinia	www.corsicaferries.com
Siremar	Islands of Sicily	www.siremar.it
SNAV	Aeolian Islands, Croatia	www.snav.it
Toremar	Tuscan Islands	www.toremar.it
Tirrenia	Sardinia, Sicily	www.terrenia.it

Guidebooks and Online Travel Resources

Italian Tourist Board	www.italiantourism.com
Slow Travelers Italy	www.slowtrav.com
Venere.com	www.venere.com
Initaly	www.initaly.com
Blue Guides	www.acblack.com
Cadogan Guides	www.cadoganguides.com
Eyewitness Travel Guides: Italy	www.dk.com
Fodor's	www.fodors.com
Frommer's	www.frommers.com
Karen Brown's Guides	www.karenbrown.com
Rick Steves	www.ricksteves.com
TimeOut	www.timeout.com
Let's Go	www.letsgo.com
Lonely Planet	www.lonelyplanet.com
Rough Guides	www.roughguides.com
Bed and Blessings	www.bedandblessings.com
Lodging in Italy's Monasteries	www.monasteriesofitaly.com

Holidays and Annual Events

In addition to the official holidays of New Year's Day, Easter, and Christmas Day, Italy also celebrates the following national holidays, when tourist sites, shops and businesses will be closed and transportation services overloaded:

Jan 6 (Epiphany)	May 20 (Ascension day)
Apr 25 (Liberation Day)	Aug 15 (Ferragosto)
May 1 (Labor Day)	Nov 1 (All Saints Day)
Monday after Easter	Dec 8 (Immaculate Conception)
	Dec 26 (Day after Christmas)

For local and regional events, see

www.hastetler.net   www.whatsgoingon.com
www.festivals.com

Internet Points (chains)
cafe.ecs.net
www.netgate.it
www.easyinternetcafe.com/map
www.made-in-italy.com/travel/cybercafes/
www.internettrain.it
www.nethousecafes.com

Internet Service (free in Italy; cost of phone call only)
www.caltanet.it
www.libero.it
www.tiscalinet.it
www.kataweb.com
www.fastweb.com

Italian Tourist Information   See *Guidebooks and Travel Resources*

Language Instruction
We recommend starting early and using as many approaches as you can combine, devoting only a little time each day, whether it's reviewing exercises in a workbook, listening to a recorded lesson in the car, or just reviewing pronunciation. Here are some programs we're confident in recommending:

Pimsleur Language Pgms
In-depth and quick-start versions.

See It and Say It In Italian   Margarita Madrigal
A great supplement to any other language program.

Italian in 10 Minutes a Day   Kristine K. Kershul
We really like her multi-faceted approach: book, stickers, flash cards, and more.

Speedy Italian   Babe Hart
A handy flip-style phrase finder.

Speak Italian with Michel Thomas
Unusual approach on CDs. Do get the deluxe version.

About Italian Language   italian.about.com
A bottomless pit of (free) ways to learn and practice the Italian language, beginning to advanced.

Maps & Driving
For countryside driving, it's essential to purchase one or more good maps with an appropriate scale for the detail you need.

Provincial maps at 50,000:1 are ideal; but regional maps (Magellan, Touring Club Italiano) at 200,000:1 are also good for combining good detail and an overall view.

Maps, regional, provincial, city   www.trektools.com

Online maps & directions   www.viamichelin.com
www.mappy.com

Autostrade info   www.autostrade.it

Money
ATM locations   www.visa.com/pd/atm/main.html
www.mastercard.com/cardholderservices/atm/

Online Currency Convertion   xe.com, oanda.com

Passport Information
US Gov   travel.state.gov/passport/
Passport Application Locations   visa.his.com
Passport Expediters   www.uspassportbureau.com
The Visa Lady   www.visalady.com

Recommended Films (Name, Director)
1900 (1976)   Bernardo Bertolucci
The Bicycle Thief (1947)   Vittorio Di Sica
Cinema Paradiso (1989)   Giuseppe Tornatore
Ciao, Professore! (1993)   Lina Wertmüller
Death In Venice (1971)   Luchino Visconti
La Dolce Vita (1960)   Federico Fellini
Enchanted April (1992)   Mike Newell
Everybody's Fine (1990)   Giuseppe Tornatore
La Grande Guerra (1959)   Mario Monicelli
The Leopard (1963)   Luchino Visconti
Malèna (2000)   Giuseppe Tornatore
Pane e Tulipani (Bread and Tulips, 2000)   Silvia Soldini
Il Postino (The Postman, 1994)   Michael Radford
Roman Holiday (1957)   William Wyler
A Room With A View (1985)   James Ivory

Tea with Mussolini (1999)	Franco Zeffirelli
La Vita è Bella (Life Is Beautiful, 2000)	Roberto Benigni

Recommended Reading (A very brief list)

A Traveler In Southern Italy	H.V. Morton
Any Four Women Could Rob a Bank in Italy	A. Cornellson
Bella Figura: A Field Guide to the Italian Mind	B. Severgnini
Brunelleschi's Dome	Ross King
Desiring Italy (collected writings)	Teresa Neunzig Cahill
Innocents Abroad	Mark Twain
Italian Days	Barbara Grizzuti Harrison
Italian Hours	Henry James
Italian Stories (dual language)	Robert A. Hall
The Italian Way	Costantino and Gambello
The Italians	Luigi Barzini
Italy In Mind: An Anthology	Alice Leccese Powers
The Leopard	Giuseppe Lampedusa
New Italian Women: A Collection of Short Fiction	
	Martha King (Editor)
The Stone Boudoir	Theresa Maggio
A Traveler's History of Italy	Valerio Lintner
Donna Leon Venetian mystery series	
Venice Observed	Mary McCarthy
Venetian Stories	Jane Turner Rylands
The World of Venice	Jan Morris

Shipping Services (All phone numbers are toll-free.)

UPS	800 877 877	www.ups.com
Fedex	800 123 800	www.fedex.com
DHL	199 199 345	www.dhl-usa.com

Tax (VAT) Refunds www.traveltax.msu.edu
www.globalrefund.com
www.premiertaxfree.com

Temperature Converter see Conversions: Temperature

Time and Date, Number Formats

March 6, 2003	is written as	06/03/03
10:10 p.m.	is written as	22.10
$1,200.00	is written as	1.200,00

Train/Rail Pass Sample Fare Comparisons

Days	Type	Rail Pass	Per day	ES Suppl.
4	1st Class	$266	$66	€11
	2nd Class	$189	$47	€8
7	1st Class	$283	$40	€11
	2nd Class	$228	$33	€8

	1st	2nd
Venice-Rome (ES)	€65	€45
Milan-Florence (ES)	€42	€29
Florence-Rome (ES)	€42	€29
Rome-Orvieto (IC)	€18	€14
Florence-Lucca (R)		€5

Train Schedules & Ticketing

TrenItalia	www.trenitalia.com
DieBahn	reiseauskunft.bahn.de/bin/query.exe/en
RailEurope	www.railEurope.com
Railpass Express	www.railpass.com
Viaggiatreno	viaggiatreno.it
Thomas Cook European Timetable	

Travel Insurance

Insure My Trip	insuremytrip.com	800 487 4722
Travel Guard	travelguard.com	800 826 1300
Travel Insured Int.	travelinsured.com	800 243 3174
Travelex Insurance	travelex-insurance.com	800 228 9792

Travel Time and Cost Estimates

Drive times are calculated at 110 km/hr (68 mph); road conditions may increase the time en route. Fuel costs are estimated at ,10 per km. Train fares are Eurostar (Standard) with durations applying to the fastest train available, no connections, unless otherwise noted. Connections and different trains will cause times and fares to vary. At this writing, AV fares with shorter transit times are available Roma-Napoli, Miilano-Torino, with more on the way.

From	To	DISTANCE		BY CAR		BY TRAIN		
		km	Miles	Time	Tolls	Time	2nd	1st
MILANO	Venezia	295	185	2:50	€13	2:31	€21	€29
	Firenze	320	200	3:00	€15	2:45	€29	€42
	Roma	630	390	6:30	€27	4:30	€46	€67
	Torino	142	88	2:00	€8	1:22	€15	€20
	Vernazza (C.Terre)	235	145	3+ hrs	€12	3:20 ICplus/ D	€20	€26
VENEZIA S.L.	Firenze	260	160	2:30	€13	2:51	€27	€39
	Roma	570	350	5:30	€25	4:36	€45	€67
	Bari	810	500	8:40	€39	8:22	€60	€85
FIRENZE	Roma	310	192	3:00	€12	1:35	€29	€42
	Napoli	490	320	5:00	€22	3:35	€42	€63
	Bari	700	435	6:40	€34	6:44	€55	€76
ROMA	Napoli	220	135	2:10	€9	1:53	€22	€37
	Bari	435	270	4:45	€18	4:37	€36	€51
MESSINA	Palermo	230	142	2:30	€6	3:15 ICplus	€16	€24
	Siracusa	165	102	2:10	€3	3:30 IC	€13	€18

VOCABULARY

@ sign	chiocciola
above	sopra
on	su
abroad	all'estero
acceptance	accetazione
admitted	ammessi
after-dinner drink	digestivo
afternoon	pomeriggio
aged	stagionato
airline company	campagnia aerea
airmail	via aerea
airplane	aereo
airport	aeroporto
alcohol	alcool
alcoholic	alcoolico
allergic	allergico
almonds	mandorle
anchovies	acciughe
another	un altro
answer	rispondere
appetizers	antipasti
apple	mele
approach	approdo
apricot	albicocca
arrival / arrivals	arrivo / arrivi
arrives	arriva
artichokes	carciofi
arugula	rucola
asparagus	asparagi

ATM, cash machine	Bancomat
available	disponibile
bag	bagaglio
bakery	panificio
bank	banca
bath	bagno
bath outside room	bagno esterno
beans	fagioli
beautiful	bello / bellissimo
beef	manzo
beer	birra
backward, behind	indietro
belt	centura
best	buonissimo
beverages, drinks	bevande, bibite
bicycle	bicicletta
big	grande
the bill	il conto
blankets	coperti
blueberry	mirtillo
boiled	bollito
bookstore	libreria
bottle	bottiglia
bottled water	minerale
box	scatola
bread	pane
breakfast	colazione
bus	autobus
bus stop	fermata
button	tasto
buy	comprare

caffeine	caffeina
car	macchina
car (train)	carozza
carbonated	frizzante
cash	contante
cell phone (colloq.)	telefonino
certainly	certo
change (money)	il resto
cheese	formaggio
cherries	ciliege
chicken	pollo
chocolate	cioccolato
city	città
closing day	giorno di chiusura
cocktail	aperitivo
cooked	cotto
coins, change	moneta
coins, change (colloq.)	spiccioli
cold	freddo
cone	cono
confirmation	conferma
connection	collegamento
a cook	cuoco
to cook	cuocere
corridor	corridoio
the cover	il coperto
Could I...?	Potrei...?
counter	sportello
course; route	corsa
cream	panna
credit card	carta di credito

currency	valuta	early, soon	presto	free (not taken)	libero
cuisine	cucina	earrings	orecchini	fresh	fresca
cup (of coffee)	tazza	east	est	juice	spremuta
cup (of ice cream)	coppa	eat	mangiare	fried	fritto
daily	giornalmente	egg	uova	fruit	frutta
day	giorno	elevator	ascensore	full-bodied (wine)	corposo
delicious	delizioso	entrance	ingresso, entrata	garage	garage
department store	grande magazzino	equal (the same)	uguale	gas station	benzinaio
departs	parte	espresso	caffè	gasoline	benzina
departure	partenza	evening	sera	get gas	fare la benzina
deposit	capparra,	exceptional	eccezionale	get off	scendere
	cauzione	exchange (rate)	cambio	get on (train or bus)	salire
desserts	dolci	exit	uscita	glass	bicchiere
destination	destinazione	expensive	caro	gloves	guanti
diabetes	diabete	expiration	scadenza	gluten	glutine
diesel	gasolio	expired (card value)	scaduto	good	buono
dinner	cena	far	lontano	Good evening.	Buonsera.
direction	direzione	fare	tariffa	Good morning.	Buongiorno.
directions (instructions)	indicazioni	fast	veloce	Goodbye.	Arrivederci.
discount	sconto	ferry	traghetto	grape harvest	vendemmia
dollars	dollari	fill it up	il pieno	grapefuit	pompelmo
door	porta	film	pellicola	grilled	alla griglia
dot	punto	the first	la prima	grocery store	alimentari
double bed	letto matrimoniale	fish	pesce	hair dryer	asciugacapelli
double room	camera doppia	flight	volo	half hour	mezz'ora
download	scaricare	fog	nebbia	ham	prosciutto
dress	vestito	forbidden	vietato	hang up (phone)	riagganciare
drink	bere	fork	forchetta	hat	cappello
drinks	bibite	forward	avanti	hazelnut	nocciola
dry cleaners	lavasecco	(in) front of	davanti	heated	scaldato
duration	durata	free (no cost)	gratis	here (it is, you are)	ecco

here / there	*qui / là*	late	*in ritardo*	morning	*mattina*
holiday	*festivo*	later	*più tardi*	motor scooter	*motorino*
holidays	*giorni festivi*	laundry	*lavanderia*	motorcycle	*moto*
hot	*caldo*	left / right	*destra / sinistra*	mushrooms	*funghi*
hot chocolate	*cioccolata calda*	lemon	*limone*	napkin	*tovagliolo*
hot tea	*tè caldo*	less	*meno*	near	*vicino*
hotel	*albergo*	letter	*lettera*	necklace	*catena*
hour / hours	*ora / ore*	lettuce	*lattuga*	newsstand	*edicola*
house wine	*vino della casa*	license plate	*targa*	next	*prossima*
hunger	*fame*	light	*leggero*	night / nights	*notte / notti*
hydrofoil	*aliscafo*	line	*linea*	no	*no*
ice	*ghiaccio*	line (traffic back up)	*coda, fila*	no parking	*divieto di sosta*
ice cream	*gelato*	a little	*poco*	no vacancy	*completo*
in effect (operates)	*si effettua*	a lot	*molto, tanto*	none	*niente, nulla*
In fact.	*Infatti.*	long	*lungo*	noon	*mezzogiorno*
in front of / behind	*davanti / indietro*	lost luggage	*bagagli smarriti*	north	*nord*
insured	*assicurata*	lunch	*pranzo*	now	*ora*
intermediate stop	*ind. suss.*	M'am	*Signora*	number	*numero*
international		Miss	*Signorina*	O.K.	*Va bene.*
express mail	*EMS*	mail box	*buca delle lettere*	oil	*olio*
international	*scheda telefonica*	map	*cartina, piantina*	omelette	*frittata*
phone card	*internazionale*	maybe	*forse*	on tap	*alla spina*
Internet point	*punto d'Internet*	meat	*carne*	opposite side	*dall'altra parte*
Internet salon	*sala d'Internet*	menu	*menù*	one-way (street)	*senso unico*
iron	*ferro da stiro*	message	*messaggio*	one-way (ticket)	*corsa semplice,*
jacket	*giacca*	midnight	*mezzanotte*		*solo andata*
jewelry	*gioielli*	milk, dairy	*latte*	operator	*operatore*
juice	*succo*	minute / minutes	*minuto / minuti*	orange	*arancia*
key	*chiave*	mixed	*misto*	overcoat	*cappotto*
knife	*coltello*	money	*soldi, denaro*	package	*pacco*
last	*ultima*	more	*di più, ancora*	packing material	*imballaggio*

paid parking	parcheggio a pagamento	purchase	acquistare	shoes	scarpe
pants, slacks	pantaloni	purse	borsa	shop	negozio, bottega
parking lot	parcheggio	rail station	ferrovia	short	corto
passengers	passeggeri	rain	pioggia	shower	doccia
pay	pagare	raspberry	lampone	side dishes	contorni
payment	pagamento	raw	crudo	sign	cartello
peach	pesca	receipt	scontrino	signal	segnale
peanuts	arachidi	red wine	vino rosso	single room	camera singola
pen	penna	reimbursement	rimborso	sir, mister	signore
pencil	matita	rent (a car)	noleggiare	size	misura
pepper	pepe	reservation	prenotazione	skirt	gonna
perfect	perfetto	rice	riso	slow	lento
permission (to pass)	permesso	right / left	destra / sinistra	small	piccolo
pharmacy	farmacia	road	strada	smoke	fumare
phone call	chiamata	roasted	arrosto	smoked (I.e., ham)	fumicato
phone card	scheda telefonica	a room	una camera	snack	spuntino
pillows	guanciali	round-trip	andata e ritorno	snow	neve
pineapple	ananas	safety	sicurezza	soup	zuppa
place	posto	sage and butter	salvia e burro	south	sud
plate	piatto	salad greens	insalata	soy	soia
platorm (train)	binario	sale	saldo	special offer	in offerta
please	per favore	salt	sale	ship	spedire
Pleased to meet you.	Molto piacere.	scarf	sciarpa	spicy	piccante
porters	portobagagli, fachini	schedule, timetable	orario	spinach	spinaci
		scratch and park	gratta e sosta	splendid	splendida
		sea	mare	spoon	cucchiaio
postcard	cartolina	seafood	frutti di mare	stamp (a ticket)	timbrare
potatoes	patate	seat	sedia	stamps	francobolli
press (button)	premere, premete	service	servizio	station	stazione
price	prezzo	shirt, blouse	camicia	steak	bistecca
prohibited	proibito, divieto	shirt (knit)	maglie	stop (train/bus)	fermata

English	Italian	English	Italian	English	Italian
store	negozio	toilette paper	carta igenica	very strong (wine)	generoso
straight	diritto	toll-free number	numero verde	voice mail	segreteria telefonica
strawberry	fragole	tomatoes	pomodori		
street	via, viale	tomorrow	domani	voyage, trip	viaggio
strike	sciopero	tomorrow evening	domani sera	wait	attendere
strong	forte	tonight	stanotte	wait one moment	un attimo solo
stupendous	stupende	too (also)	anche	waiting for (bus)	in attesa
sugar	zucchero	too (much)	troppo	wallet	portafoglio
surface shipping	pacco ordinario	towels	asciugamani	water	acqua
table	un tavolo	track (train)	binario	watermelon	anguria, cocomero
talk	parlare	traffic light	semaforo	weather	tempo
tap water	dal rubinetto	train	treno	Web page	pagina Web
tea	tè	train information	informazioni treni	weekdays	giorni lavorativi, giorni feriali
telephone	telefono	travel agency	agenzia di viaggi		
Thank you.	Grazie.	trip, voyage	viaggio	west	ovest
that / this	quello / questo	triple room	camera tripla	What is...	Cos'è...
then	poi	t-shirt, vest	maglietta	What	Che cosa?
thirst	sete	tunnel	galleria	when	Quando
this / that	questo / quello	twin beds	letti separati	Where is...	Dov'è...
this evening	stasera	post office	ufficio postale	where	dove
ticket (beel-yet-toh)	biglietto	under	sotto	which	quale
ticket for one ride	biglietto ordinario	unleaded (gas)	benzina verde, senza piombo	Who knows.	Chissà.
ticket vendor	biglietteria			Who?	Chi?
tie	cravatta	up / down	su / giù	Why? (Because...)	Perchè? (Perchè...)
tight	stretto	urban, metro	urbana	window	finestra
time	tempo	validate	coinvalidare	wine	vino
tip	la mancia	vanilla	crema	wine tasting	degustazione
tires	gomme	veg. accompaniment	contorni	yes	sì
tissues	fazzoletti	vegetables	verdure	yesterday	ieri
today	oggi	vegetarian	vegetariano	you're welcome	prego
toilette	toilette	very good	molto buono	zucchini	zucchine

For bulk sales and distribution information, please contact

Beagle Bay Books
beaglebay.com   775.827.8654

For individual sales contact Amazon.com, any bookseller near you,
or our web site (downloads, podcasts, and more):

italyinstructions.com